Fashion Pioneer

JEANNE LANVIN

Visionärin der Mode

PIERRE TOROMANOFF

Fashion Pioneer

JEANNE LANVIN

Visionärin der Mode

teNeues

Contents

Inhalt

Introduction

To paraphrase one of Voltaire's most famous sentences, if Jeanne Lanvin had not existed, her life could not have been invented, for it is so full of unexpected turns and resounding successes that it challenges imagination. Like the tale of a thousand and one nights, it is an extraordinary story in a thousand and one dresses, a thousand and one hats, coats and accessories. It is the life of a genius dedicated to fashion encompassing more than half a century of collections, which were always fresh, always surprising, and magnificent, and whose splendour still dazzles us many decades later.

The extraordinary destiny of this child born into a family that was as numerous as it was poor, who was placed in an apprenticeship at the age of thirteen and who, through her unmatched strength of will, exceptional intellectual curiosity and extraordinary tenacity, founded and directed a house of haute couture, and was befriended by the most exquisite minds of her time can only but arouse our admiration. The visionary and pioneering spirit that animated Jeanne Lanvin throughout her life is, however, even more remarkable: She was the first high fashion designer to open a children's department and to explore sportswear. She even extended her activities to interior design, thus opening up fashion to lifestyle. Her artworks – for her designs deserve to be called works of art – range from wedding dresses to theatrical costumes and from exuberantly ornamented hats to evening gowns inspired by the clean lines of Art Deco. She designed perfumes, accessories, and fur coats, with the same uncompromising commitment to perfection, as evidenced by the magnificence of the embroideries and the elegance of the cuts.

While other couturiers, such as Paul Poiret, Coco Chanel and Elsa Schiaparelli, have changed the history of fashion by breaking away from certain codes or by playing the provocateur, Jeanne Lanvin transformed fashion without seeking to revolutionise it. But at the same time, she also supported the social changes of that period: she dressed ladies of the Belle Époque as well as those of the immediate post-WWII period with the same elegance, and her only aim was to magnify women.
Her outfits for the emancipated *garçonnes* of the 1920s were just as subtle and original as her signature *robes de style* of the same decade, a style she was particularly fond of, and continued to design even when their popularity waned.
Nothing seemed impossible to Jeanne Lanvin, including the invention of new colours that are today associated with the brand she founded: Lanvin blue, of course, but also Polignac pink, created as a tribute to her daughter Marguerite, as well as many other delicate hues. In the Roaring Twenties, she did not hesitate to open a dye factory since her desire for perfection prompted her to overcome any barriers that stood in her way.
Inspired by an endless variety of sources, Jeanne Lanvin was skilled at instinctively assimilating and reinterpreting the most diverse influences and motifs, from Aztec patterns to Slavic embroidery and orientalism, and from the fashion of the French *ancien régime* to cubism. Her talent still resonates today.

A *catalogue raisonné* may one day reveal the full extent of her genius: Jeanne Lanvin is to haute couture and fragrances what Leonardo da Vinci is to painting and science. The purpose of this book is to lift the veil on her prodigious oeuvre,

Édouard Vuillard.
Jeanne Lanvin, 1933.

Édouard Vuillard.
Jeanne Lanvin, 1933.

to show her masterpieces, and to highlight the avant-garde spirit that animated this woman. Naturally silent and modest, and enraged by her inability to draw – a strange situation for a fashion designer – not only did she count the most brilliant playwrights and writers of her time among her friends, but also collected art.

Moreover, her life is the tale of a woman who overcame adversity and social determinism, demonstrated formidable business acumen, and defied the conventions of the time to live as she saw fit. As such, she serves as an example and inspiration to all women.

Vorwort

Frei nach Voltaire würde man sagen: Ein Leben wie das von Jeanne Lanvin kann man sich nicht ausdenken. Ihre Geschichte steckt so voller unerwarteter Wendungen und riesiger Erfolge, dass sie die Fantasie bisweilen übersteigt. Es ist eine Geschichte so außergewöhnlich wie die Märchen aus Tausendundeiner Nacht – wobei hier allerdings tausendundein Kleider, Mäntel und Accessoires die Hauptrolle spielen. Jeanne Lanvin war ein Genie: Ein halbes Jahrhundert lang entwarf sie Kollektionen, die stets überraschten, stets für frischen Wind sorgten, und dabei so wunderschön waren, dass sie uns viele Jahre später noch begeistern.

Clémentine-Hélène Dufau. *Jeanne Lanvin*, 1925.

Clémentine-Hélène Dufau. *Jeanne Lanvin*, 1925.

Jeanne Lanvins außerordentliches Schicksal kann uns nur ins Staunen versetzen: Ein Mädchen aus armer, kinderreicher Familie geht mit nur 13 Jahren in die Lehre und schafft es dank ihrer immensen Willenskraft, großer Neugier und Hartnäckigkeit, ein Modehaus für Haute Couture zum Erfolg zu führen. Ihr Freundeskreis bestand aus den klügsten Köpfen ihrer Zeit. Noch bemerkenswerter ist allerdings ihre ständige Vorreiterrolle. Sie war die erste Haute-Couture-Schöpferin, die eine Abteilung für Kinderkleidung schuf und sich an Sportkleidung heranwagte. Sogar in den Bereich der Inneneinrichtung wagte sie sich vor. Die große Bandbreite ihrer Kunst – und als solche kann man ihr Schaffen durchaus bezeichnen – umfasst Brautkleider ebenso wie Kostüme fürs Theater und reicht vom üppig verzierten Hut bis zum geradlinigen Abendkleid im Stile des Art déco. Ob Parfum, Accessoire oder Pelzmantel: Sie strebte bei all ihren Kreationen nach Perfektion, wie sich in den eleganten Formen und herrlichen Stickereien zeigt. Während Modeschöpfer wie Paul Poiret, Coco Chanel oder Elsa Schiaparelli die Mode für immer veränderten, indem sie provokant auftraten oder sich von der Norm entfernten, bewirkte Jeanne Lanvin einen Wandel in der Mode, den sie nie vorgehabt hatte. Und dennoch unterstützte sie mit ihrem Schaffen die gesellschaftlichen Veränderungen der Zeit. Sie kleidete die Damen der Belle Époque ebenso elegant ein wie die Frauen der Nachkriegszeit. Ihr Ziel war es dabei stets, Frauen zu bestärken. Ihre Entwürfe für die emanzipierten *Garçonnes* der 1920er Jahre waren ebenso subtil und originell wie ihre charakteristische *Robe de style*, die im gleichen Jahrzehnt entstand. Diese Kleider liebte sie besonders und entwarf sie auch dann noch, als deren Beliebtheit bereits abnahm. Für Jeanne Lanvin schien nichts unmöglich zu sein. So kreierte sie auch neue Farben, die bis heute mit der Marke in Verbindung gebracht werden   Lanvin-Blau, Polignac-Rosa, das sie ihrer Tochter Marguerite widmete, und viele weitere sanfte Nuancen. In den Goldenen Zwanzigern eröffnete sie sogar eine eigene Färberei, um sicherzugehen, dass sie genau die gewünschten Farbtöne erhalten würde. Jeanne Lanvin ließ sich aus zahlreichen Quellen inspirieren und hatte ein Talent dafür, verschiedenste Einflüsse und Motive für sich anzupassen und neu zu interpretieren, vom Aztekenmuster über slawische Stickerei bis hin zu orientalischen Einflüssen, von der Mode des *Ancien Régime* bis zum Kubismus. Ihre außerordentliche Gabe wirkt bis in die heutige Zeit nach.

Sollten eines Tages ihre gesammelten Werke veröffentlicht werden, würde das gesamte Ausmaß ihres Schaffens deutlich. Denn Jeanne Lanvin war für die Haute Couture und die Welt des Parfums so wichtig wie Leonardo da Vinci für die Malerei und Wissenschaft. Ziel dieses Buches ist es, den Schleier über ihre Kreationen zu lüften, so dass ihr umfassendes, vorausschauendes Werk und ihre zahlreichen Meisterwerke bewundert werden können.
Jeanne Lanvin war eine ruhige, bescheidene Frau. Was sie allerdings erzürnte, war die Tatsache, nicht gut zeichnen zu können – eine in der Tat sehr ungewöhnliche Eigenschaft für eine Modeschöpferin. Dazu war sie Kunstsammlerin und zählte die klügsten Künstler und Schriftsteller der Zeit zu ihren Freunden. Vor allem ist ihr Leben aber die Geschichte einer Frau, die es trotz aller Widerstände und gesellschaftlicher Starrheit zu Erfolg brachte und sich den Konventionen ihrer Zeit widersetzte, wann immer das notwendig war. Als diese Vorreiterin ist sie vielen Frauen auch heute noch Vorbild und Inspiration.

1867-1884

A dreamless childhood

Eine Kindheit ohne Träume

At the dawn of 1867, the reign of Emperor Napoléon III was reaching its zenith, and a renovated, modernized Paris was preparing to welcome the seventh *Exposition Universelle d'art et d'industrie*, which would host more than fifty thousand exhibitors and ten million visitors from early April to late October, including German Emperor William I, his powerful chancellor Otto von Bismarck, the Prince of Wales, the Russian Tsar Alexander II, and Turkish Sultan Abdülaziz. At the Emperor's instigation, the Prefect of Paris, Georges Eugène Haussmann, had ordered the complete demolition of several old, poorly maintained districts, which were replaced by beautiful avenues lined with elegant, modern buildings, thus paving the way for the "city of light", a name that Paris would rightly deserve during the Belle Époque. Jeanne, the first daughter of Sophie Blanche and Bernard Constant Lanvin, would thus come into the world on the first day of a year marked by art, industry, and modernity.

Paradoxically, the wind of progress had not reached her birthplace, at 35 rue Mazarine, in the heart of the old Paris, just a stone's throw away from the Seine's left embankment. The area, located in the immediate vicinity of the Académie Française, was populated by literate workers, such as Jeanne's father, who was a low-ranking employee at various printing presses nearby. As shown in Eugène Atget's photographs, which were made a few years later, the narrow rue Mazarine was not at all a Haussmann-style boulevard. It was a street of overgrown buildings inhabited by poor workers' families, who would often be won over by the ideas of Pierre-Joseph Proudhon, whose libertarian socialist theories would serve as the inspiration for the establishment of the Paris Commune three years later.

Anfang des Jahres 1867, auf dem Höhepunkt der Herrschaft Kaiser Napoleons III, bereitete sich das modernisierte Paris gerade mit Hochdruck auf die siebte Weltausstellung vor. Mehr als 50 000 Aussteller und zehn Millionen Besucher, darunter der deutsche Kaiser Wilhelm I, sein einflussreicher Kanzler Otto von Bismarck, der britische Thronfolger, der russische Zar Alexander II und der türkische Sultan Abdülaziz wurden zwischen April und Oktober erwartet. Auf Geheiß Kaiser Napoleons hatte der damalige Pariser Präfekt, Georges Eugène Haussmann, angeordnet, alte Stadtviertel in schlechtem Zustand niederzureißen. An ihre Stelle traten prächtige Straßen, die von eleganten, modernen Gebäuden gesäumt wurden und Paris in die „Stadt der Lichter" verwandelten – ein Name, dem die Großstadt während der Belle Époque mehr als gerecht werden würde. Und so wurde Jeanne am 1. Januar in ein Jahr geboren, das in besonderer Weise von Kunst, Industrie und Moderne geprägt sein sollte.

An Jeannes Geburtsort, der Rue Mazarine Nummer 35 im Herzen des alten Paris, nur einen Steinwurf vom linken Seineufer entfernt, war von den Fortschritten wenig zu spüren. Hier, in unmittelbarer Nähe zur Académie Française, lebten Arbeiter wie Jeannes Vater, der sein Geld als einfacher Angestellter in den Druckereien des Quartiers verdiente. Wie die Jahre später aufgenommenen Fotografien von Eugène Atget zeigen, war die schmale Rue Mazarine alles andere als ein Haussmann-Boulevard: In den überwucherten Häusern lebten arme Arbeiterfamilien, von denen viele den Ideen Pierre-Joseph Proudhons anhingen, dessen anarchistischer Sozialismus drei Jahre später maßgeblich zur Bildung der Pariser Kommune beitrug.

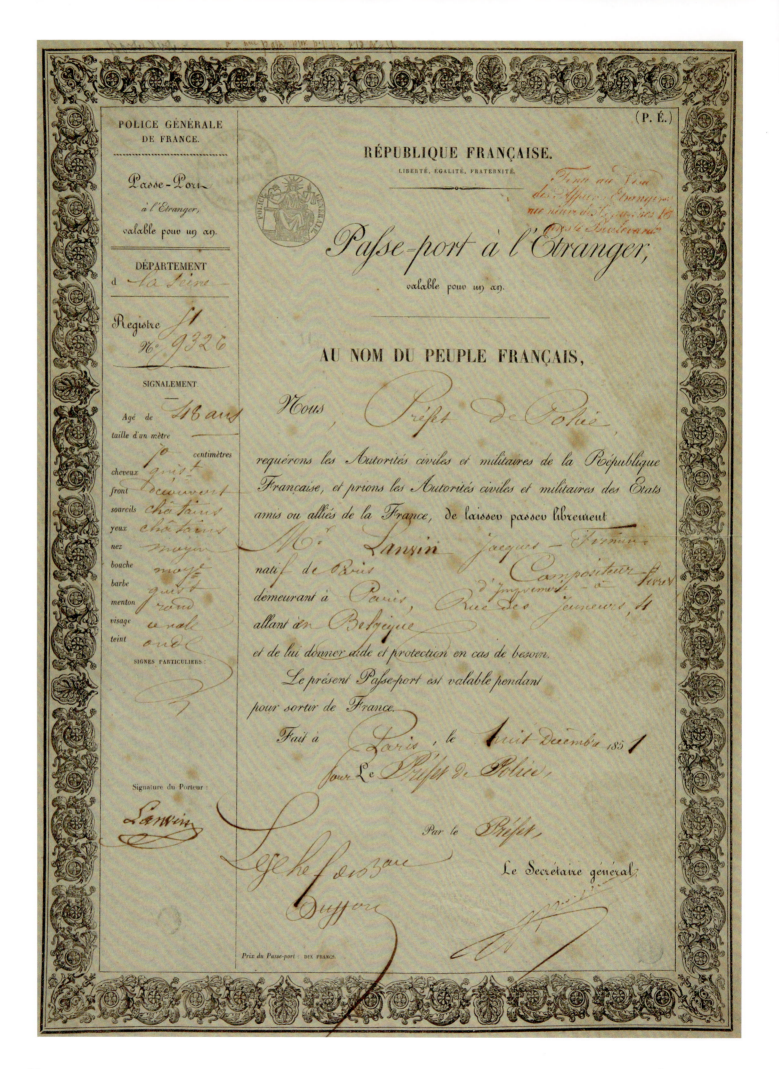

Jeanne's paternal grandfather, Jacques Firmin Lanvin, had achieved some fame in 1851, during Louis-Napoléon Bonaparte's presidential *coup d'état*, by helping a famous opponent of the future emperor flee to Belgium: Victor Hugo. By lending his passport to the poet and writer whom he had befriended, Jacques Lanvin had enabled the author of *The Hunchback of Notre-Dame* to escape from France, where he was a wanted man. Victor Hugo felt a debt of gratitude towards this literate, politically committed worker, and tirelessly supported the Lanvin family through a number of crises when he was able to return to France after the Empire had been overthrown. For Jeanne Lanvin's early years were anything but a fairy tale: the siege of Paris during the Franco-Prussian war of 1870-1871, followed by the upheaval of the Commune, had brought famine and misery to the poorest Parisian classes. As if these misfortunes were not enough, Jeanne's father, Bernard Constant, despite his middle name, proved to be inconstant at work, changing employers frequently, presumably due to alcoholism that was widespread in the working class at the time. These circumstances, despite the help regularly provided by Victor Hugo, weighed heavily on the steadily expanding family. In addition to Jeanne, born in 1867, the couple gave birth to eight boys and two girls between 1868 and 1881. As a result, the Lanvins were gradually forced to leave the centre of Paris for the outskirts, and then the suburbs, to accommodate this large family, even while their financial situation was clearly not improving. As a consequence of these hardships, Jeanne acquired an acute sense of responsibility at an early age, taking care of her siblings to relieve her mother, who was always pregnant or breastfeeding, and she faced the reality of a destitute existence instead of enjoying a childhood lulled by dreams and carefree days. With such a background, one could see the possible origins of her perpetually busy, work-focused mind, and of her devotion to the family; in fact some of her brothers, nieces, and nephews would join the company she founded.

Als Präsident Louis-Napoléon Bonaparte 1851 zum Staatsstreich angesetzt hatte, war Jeannes Großvater väterlicherseits, Jacques Firmin Lanvin, zu einer kleinen Berühmtheit geworden, weil er Victor Hugo, einem berühmten Gegner des künftigen Kaisers, bei der Flucht nach Belgien half. Er hatte dem befreundeten Schriftsteller seinen Pass geliehen, wodurch dem Autor von „Der Glöckner von Notre-Dame" die Flucht aus Frankreich gelang, obwohl fieberhaft nach ihm gefahndet wurde. Als Victor Hugo nach dem Sturz des Kaisers nach Frankreich zurückkehrte, tat er sich als unermüdlicher Unterstützer der Familie hervor, da er in tiefer Dankbarkeit mit dem belesenen, politisch aktiven Arbeiter Lanvin verbunden war. Und Gelegenheit zur Unterstützung gab es reichlich, denn Jeannes Kindheit verlief alles andere als märchenhaft. Auf die Belagerung von Paris während des deutsch-französischen Krieges 1870-1871 folgten die Unruhen der Pariser Kommune, so dass in den ärmeren Schichten Hunger und Elend herrschten. Dazu kam, dass Jeannes Vater, Bernard Constant Lanvin, die Familie mit seiner unbeständigen Arbeit immer wieder ins

Ungewisse stürzte. Die häufig wechselnden Anstellungen waren möglicherweise auf ein Alkoholproblem zurückzuführen, das in der Arbeiterschaft von damals weit verbreitet war. Trotz der Unterstützung durch Victor Hugo hatte es die stetig wachsende Familie unter diesen Umständen nicht leicht. Auf Jeannes Geburt 1867 folgten zwischen 1868 und 1881 noch acht Jungen und zwei weitere Mädchen. Irgendwann sah sich die Großfamilie gezwungen, vom Stadtzentrum zunächst in einen Außenbezirk und schließlich in einen Vorort zu ziehen. Ihre finanzielle Lage verbesserte sich dadurch aber nicht. Angesichts dieser Nöte begann Jeanne schon sehr früh, Verantwortung zu übernehmen. Um ihre ständig schwangere oder stillende Mutter, Sophie Blanche, zu entlasten, kümmerte sie sich tatkräftig um ihre Geschwister. Statt einer sorgenfreien Kindheit voller Träume erlebte Jeanne am eigenen Leib, was es heißt, in bitterer Armut zu leben. Vor diesem Hintergrund lässt sich leicht nachvollziehen, wie sie zu einer so rastlosen, strebsamen Person wurde, die immer für ihre Familie da war und später gleich mehrere Brüder, Nichten und Neffen in ihrer Firma einstellte.

Jeanne received a primary education at most thanks to liberal laws passed in 1867 under the influence of Victor Duruy, Napoléon III's open-minded Minister of Education, who established free elementary education for girls in major cities. The final implementation of mandatory, secular education would not happen until fifteen years later, in 1882, by his successor, Jules Ferry. Although the time Jeanne spent at school was certainly short, she did nevertheless develop a taste for reading – perhaps encouraged by the culture of the printing workers, the social environment in which she grew up. This was the first sign of the great intellectual curiosity that would animate her throughout her life and lead her to become a self-taught enthusiast of theatre, literature, music, fine arts, fabrics, and travels. The scarce contemporary reports of Jeanne's youth describe her as an assiduous reader of Émile Zola's novels and a collector of fashion illustrations. One can imagine that she found in them an escape from the gloomy world described in *L'Assommoir*, which constituted her daily life, and a first encounter, even if literary, with the upper-class world which one day would wear her most beautiful dresses. For the time being, however, Jeanne, as the eldest of eleven children, needed to contribute to the family's resources. At barely thirteen, she joined the world of labour, in the lowest rank of the hierarchy, at Madame Bonni, a Parisian milliner's house located 3 rue du Faubourg-Saint-Honoré, the same street whose name would become the symbol of Jeanne's success a few years later.

While starting an apprenticeship at a young age often meant a life of uncertainty and struggle, these first steps into the realm of fashion proved to be an unexpected opportunity for the young girl who had just left a dreamless childhood and was eager to discover the world.

Mit den liberalen Gesetzen, die 1867 unter dem Einfluss Victor Duruys, dem progressiven Bildungsminister unter Napoléon III, verabschiedet wurden, kam die kostenlose Grundschulbildung für Mädchen. So konnte auch Jeanne zumindest die Grundschule besuchen. Erst 15 Jahre später, 1882, würde Duruys Nachfolger, Jules Ferry, die verpflichtende weiterführende Schule einführen. Obwohl Jeanne nur kurz zur Schule ging, wurde sie zu einer eifrigen Leserin – möglicherweise auch dank ihres sozialen Umfelds, in dem sich viele Druckereiarbeiter tummelten. In ihrer Leidenschaft für Bücher zeigte sich zum ersten Mal ihr großes intellektuelles Interesse, das sie ein Leben lang begleiten sollte und sich in einer großen Begeisterung für das Theater, die Literatur, die Kunst, das Reisen und schöne Stoffe niederschlagen würde. In den wenigen Zeitberichten aus ihrer Jugend wird sie als emsige Leserin von Émile Zolas Romanen und als Sammlerin von Modebildern beschrieben. Die Geschichten und Bilder waren für sie wohl wie eine Flucht aus dem düsteren echten Leben, wie es in Zolas *Totschläger* beschrieben wird, und gleichzeitig eine – wenn auch nur literarische – erste Begegnung mit jener Oberschicht, die später ihre Kleider tragen würde. Als ältestes von elf Kindern musste Jeanne jedoch zunächst zum Familieneinkommen beitragen. Mit gerade mal 13 Jahren nahm sie deshalb eine Stelle bei der Pariser Hutmacherin Madame Bonni in der Rue du Faubourg-Saint-Honoré an – eben jener Straße, die Jahre später zu *dem* Symbol ihres Erfolgs werden würde.

Eine Lehre in so jungen Jahren bedeutete zwar, dass Jeannes Leben häufig von Mühen und Unsicherheit geprägt war. Die ersten Schritte in die Modewelt sollten sich für das junge Mädchen jedoch als unerwartete Chance erweisen. Denn nach einer Kindheit ohne Träume blickte sie jetzt voller Neugier in die Welt hinaus.

1885-1899

A passion for hats

Eine Leidenschaft für Hüte

While today bespoke hat making is
a realm restricted to a handful of luxury
craftspeople who depend on members
of the top upper-class to make a living
from their craft, at the beginning of Belle
Époque the millinery market was at its
height. What we consider an accessory
to show off at horse races or weddings was
then an indispensable part of the social
etiquette for both women and men.
No woman, even of the humblest condition,
would go out in the street without covering
her head with an appropriate headwear.
A bareheaded woman in the street would
draw disapproving looks from passers-by
and suspicions of questionable morality
until the late 1950s. The same was true
for men, with a social distinction between
those from the wealthy classes who wore
hats and the less privileged, such as
workers, who chose caps. In Paris alone,
more than 650 milliners were established
at the beginning of the 20th century.
They therefore competed with each other
in their inventiveness to create new
models that would suit their clientele's
tastes, especially since hats displayed a
particular element of fantasy in a fashion
where women were still very corseted –
literally and figuratively. As long as you
had the means to satisfy your fantasies,
nothing prevented you from having your
hat decorated with fruit or flowers made
of ribbons, with bird feathers, with various
decorative motifs or with veils that revealed
the mood and personality of the wearer.
As each hat must be as unique, and
appropriately original as possible –
some were true Arcimboldo-like artworks –
milliners offered a dizzying array of colours,
shapes and decorative embellishments.
A flock of skilled female workers –
seamstresses, embroiderers, feather
workers, to name but a few, turn the fitting
and manufacturing of a hat into a beehive-
like ballet where each of them has
a specifically assigned task and
her place in a strict hierarchy.

p. 22: Winged hat, around 1936.

S. 22: Asymmetrischer Hut, ca. 1936.

A Parisian millinery workshop in the late 1900s.

Pariser Hutmacherwerkstatt im späten 19. Jahrhundert.

Pferderennen oder Hochzeiten Eindruck schindet, war er damals für Männer wie für Frauen ein unverzichtbarer Bestandteil der guten Etikette. Selbst Frauen aus bescheidensten Verhältnissen hätten sich ohne angemessene Kopfbedeckung nicht auf der Straße gezeigt. Eine Frau ohne Kopfbedeckung zog bis in die späten 1950er Jahre missbilligende Blicke von Passanten auf sich und man hätte wohl auch ihren Charakter angezweifelt. Bei den Männern sah es ähnlich aus, wobei hier auch der soziale Status eine Rolle spielte: Männer aus wohlhabenden Schichten trugen Hüte, Arbeiter und weniger privilegierte Männer trugen Mützen. Allein in Paris gab es Anfang des 20. Jahrhunderts mehr als 650 Hutmacher. Im ständigen Wettbewerb versuchten sie, einander mit einfallsreichen neuen Modellen zu übertrumpfen. Für Frauen waren Hüte außerdem eine Möglichkeit, ihrer Kreativität freien Lauf zu lassen und Charakter zu zeigen, denn häufig lebten sie sowohl im übertragenen als auch im wörtlichen modischen Sinne sehr eingeschnürt. Hüte gab es in allen Formen und Farben: mit Blumen oder mit aus Bändern geformten Früchten geziert, mit Federn, verschiedensten Motiven oder Schleiern. Sie alle sollten die Persönlichkeit oder Stimmung der Trägerin zum Ausdruck bringen. Wer es sich also leisten konnte, solche modischen Fantasien in die Tat umzusetzen, tat das auch. Da jeder Hut so einzigartig und originell wie möglich sein sollte – einige waren regelrechte Kunstwerke im Stile Arcimboldos – warben Hutmacher mit einer immensen Bandbreite an Farben, Formen und Verzierungen. Gefertigt wurden die Hüte schließlich von einer Schar kunstfertiger Arbeiterinnen – Näherinnen, Stickerinnen und Federkünstlerinnen –, die wie die Bienen in einem Bienenstock emsig zusammenarbeiteten, wobei jede ihre Aufgabe und ihren festen Platz in der Hierarchie hatte.

Der Markt für maßgefertigte Hüte ist heutzutage sehr überschaubar. Nur die oberen Gesellschaftsschichten kommen als Kundschaft für eine exklusive Handvoll Hutmacher in Frage. Am Anfang der Belle Époque befand sich das Hutmachergewerbe jedoch auf seinem Höhepunkt. Während der Hut in der heutigen Zeit nicht mehr als ein Accessoire ist, mit dem man bei

In this constellation of talents, Jeanne Lanvin was merely a young apprentice whose mother had probably taught her the rudiments of sewing, with perhaps a complement of practical education dispensed by one of the many religious institutions in charge of training deprived little girls. She had the status of an *arpète*, a somewhat condescending name for the young apprentices to whom all the unglamorous tasks of the workshop fell: tidying up in the mornings and evenings, collecting scraps of material, fetching everything the older workers needed. It was really the role of a dogsbody, always at the service of the entire workshop, at the mercy of pettiness and bullying. However, this poorly paid work seemed to suit the young Jeanne, who saw it as an escape from her hopeless family life. She undoubtedly took a certain pride in helping her family financially, especially since the birth of Marie-Alix in 1881, her favourite sister and the last of the siblings. One of Jeanne's frequent tasks was to deliver new hats to clients, and this activity allowed her to discover the most fashionable neighbourhoods of Paris. To save a handful of pennies on what she earned, Jeanne refrained from taking the omnibuses and instead followed their routes by running, in all seasons and weather conditions, which earned her the nickname of "little omnibus". She occasionally pocketed some tips, which added to the scant salary she brought home. Her serious nature, modesty, and dedication to work presumably earned her unanimous respect. Her zeal certainly set her above the more careless apprentices of her age, to the extent that three years later she was invited to join a more prestigious millinery, Madame Félix, at 15 rue du Faubourg-Saint-Honoré – an address that will become, a couple of decades later, Lanvin's showroom for interior design. At Madame Félix, she really got to learn the subtle art of manufacturing a hat, and her innate talent ensured her rapid promotion within the workshop. Soon, however, she decided to join yet another of the most prestigious and fashionable houses in Paris, Cordeau et Laugaudin, where she would complete her education.

Embroidery workshop, 1910s.

Verzierungsarbeiten in einer Werkstatt, 1910er Jahre.

A PASSION FOR HATS / EINE LEIDENSCHAFT FÜR HÜTE (1885-1899)

In diesem Kontext war Jeanne Lanvin lediglich ein kleines Lehrlingsmädchen, das die Grundlagen des Nähens von seiner Mutter gelernt hatte. Zusätzlich hatten ihr, wie so vielen anderen armen Mädchen auch, die verschiedenen religiösen Einrichtungen wohl ein Mindestmaß an handwerklichen Fähigkeiten vermittelt. Bei Madame Bonni hatte sie den Status einer *arpète* –

ein eher herablassender Name für die jungen Auszubildenden, denen all die weniger glamourösen Aufgaben zufielen: das morgendliche und abendliche Aufräumen, Stoffreste einsammeln, den älteren Arbeiterinnen auf Zuruf zur Verfügung stehen. Sie war im wahrsten Sinne des Wortes das Mädchen für alles, das allen in der Werkstatt stets zu Diensten sein musste, selbst wenn sie von oben herab behandelt oder gar schikaniert wurde. Dennoch schien diese schlecht bezahlte Arbeit der jungen Jeanne nicht zu missfallen, denn sie sah darin einen Ausweg aus der Hoffnungslosigkeit, die sie von zu Hause kannte. Ohne Zweifel war sie außerdem stolz darauf, ihre Familie finanziell unterstützen zu können, insbesondere nach der Geburt ihrer jüngsten Schwester Marie-Alix, die sie besonders mochte, im Jahr 1881.

Da sie häufig beauftragt wurde, neue Hüte an die Kundinnen zu liefern, konnte sie auch die schickeren Pariser Stadtviertel erkunden. Um ein paar Groschen zu sparen, ging Jeanne dabei zu Fuß, statt den Bus zu nehmen. Selbst im Winter und bei Regen durchquerte sie die Stadt im Laufschritt, was ihr den Spitznamen „kleiner Omnibus" einbrachte. Ab und zu gab es für die Lieferung etwas Trinkgeld, mit dem sie ihren mageren Lohn aufbessern konnte. Mit Ernsthaftigkeit, Bescheidenheit und Fleiß erarbeitete sie sich Respekt von allen Seiten. Dank ihres Arbeitseifers stach sie weniger beflissene Lehrlinge aus und bekam drei Jahre später eine Stelle bei einer anderen, renommierteren Hutmacherin. Das Geschäft von Madame Félix befand sich in der Rue du Faubourg-Saint-Honoré Nummer 15. Genau hier sollte Jahre später die Inneneinrichtungslinie von Jeanne Lanvin ausgestellt werden. Bei Madame Félix lernte Jeanne die künstlerischen Aspekte der Hutanfertigung kennen und stieg dank ihres Talents schnell auf. Schon bald wechselte sie zu Cordeau et Laugaudin, einem der elegantesten, prestigeträchtigsten Ateliers in ganz Paris, wo sie ihre Ausbildung abschloss.

Pierre-Auguste Renoir. *The Milliner*, 1877. Renoir portrayed a young apprentice on her way to deliver a hat to one of the boutique's clients, as Jeanne Lanvin often did in her first years of apprenticeship.

Pierre-Auguste Renoir. *Die Hutmacherin*, 1877. Renoirs Gemälde zeigt ein Lehrlingsmädchen, das sich auf den Weg macht, einen Hut an eine Kundin zu liefern, wie es auch Jeanne Lanvin in ihren ersten Lehrjahren sehr oft getan hat.

No portrait, drawing or photograph ever captured the daily work of the young Lanvin as an apprentice, but some pastels by Edgar Degas and paintings by Renoir allow us to recreate the atmosphere that reigned in the milliners' shops. *The Milliner*, painted by Renoir in 1877, shows a young apprentice carrying a hat box for delivery to the city. The pastel drawings Degas made between 1881 and 1882 – just as Jeanne began her apprenticeship – reveal a stark contrast between idle clientele who take their time trying on hats and the bustling activity of those manufacturing them.
It is difficult to say how Jeanne Lanvin felt about this clientele of aristocrats,

upper-class bourgeoisie, socialites, and courtesans, whose eternal vanity was so far away from her daily concerns, but whom she was later to meet and socialise with, even if she always kept a certain distance guided by her modest nature. Nevertheless, hats would always have a special place in her work, long after she diversified her activities and joined the exclusive circles of *haute couture*. Even when the exuberance of the Belle Époque hats gave way to more sober models inspired by Art Déco, Jeanne Lanvin remained both highly original in her hat designs and perfectly in tune with the spirit of the time.

Es gibt zwar weder Porträts noch Zeichnungen oder Fotos der jungen Jeanne Lanvin als Lehrling bei der Arbeit, doch dank künstlerischer Darstellungen von Renoir und Degas können wir uns die Stimmung, die bei den Hutmachern dieser Zeit geherrscht haben muss, lebhaft vorstellen. Renoirs Gemälde *Die Hutmacherin* von 1877 zeigt ein junges Lehrlingsmädchen mit Hutkoffer, das sich auf den Weg macht, eine Kundin zu beliefern. Die Pastellzeichnungen, die Edgar Degas zwischen 1881 und 1882 – als auch Jeanne ihre Lehre begann – anfertigte, offenbaren einen deutlichen Kontrast: auf der einen Seite steht die Kundschaft, die sich beim Anprobieren der Hüte alle Zeit der Welt lässt, auf der anderen Seite stehen jene, die unermüdlich an deren

Fertigung arbeiten. Wie Jeanne über diese Kundschaft dachte, wissen wir nicht. Die Aristokratinnen, die Damen aus der Oberschicht, Prominente und Kurtisanen, die nichts mit Jeanne und ihren täglichen Sorgen gemein hatten, wird Jeanne später noch viel näher kennenlernen. Aufgrund ihrer bescheidenen Art wahrte sie jedoch stets eine gewisse Distanz. Auch in ihrem späteren Schaffen, als Jeanne sich bereits in andere Bereiche der Mode vorgewagt hatte und in den exklusiven Kreisen der Haute Couture verkehrte, spielten Hüte für sie eine besondere Rolle. So entwarf Jeanne Lanvin auch dann noch originelle, zeitgemäße Designs, als die extravaganten Hüte der Belle Époque von schlichteren Art-déco-Modellen abgelöst worden waren.

Edgar Degas.
At the Milliner's, 1882.

Edgar Degas.
Bei der Hutmacherin,
1882.

To supplement her income, Jeanne had developed the habit of manufacturing dolls' hats from the scraps of fabric and materials she collected in the workshop. With the help of her brothers, she would sell them to toy shops. This was her first step into business, and the first time she created her own models that reflected the trends of the moment. Although she now enjoyed regular employment with Félix and then with Cordeau et Laugaudin, Jeanne was not immune to the forced and unpaid leave that employers frequently imposed on their staff during the summer: the clients were then on holiday by the seaside or at spa resorts, and this low season left the employees empty-handed and resourceless, as most were paid on a piecework basis.

Um ihr Einkommen aufzustocken, war Jeanne dazu übergegangen, aus Material- und Stoffresten Puppenhüte zu fertigen, die sie mit der Hilfe ihrer Brüder an Spielzeuggeschäfte verkaufte. So unternahm sie erste Schritte in die Geschäftswelt und kreierte erstmals eigene Modelle, die sich an den aktuellen Trends orientierten. Zwar war sie bei Madame Félix und später bei Cordeau et Laugaudin fest angestellt, doch während des Sommers musste sie wie viele andere Angestellte eine unbezahlte Zwangspause einlegen. Die Kundschaft blieb aus, da sie den Sommer am Meer oder in edlen Resorts verbrachte, so dass Angestellte der Branche, die in der Regel nach Stückzahl bezahlt wurden, währenddessen mit leeren Händen dastanden.

La Rambla, Barcelona, around 1885.

La Rambla, Barcelona, ca. 1885.

To remedy this uncomfortable situation, Jeanne decided in the summer of 1884 to accept an invitation from a Spanish lady who offered her a substantial salary to work during the summer months in Madrid, where Parisian milliners were sought after for the exquisite quality of their work. This may seem a foolish undertaking for a 17-year-old girl who had never travelled and knew no foreign language, but we must assume that Jeanne's natural curiosity drove her to try her luck. This first trip abroad turned out to be disastrous. As soon as Jeanne crossed the border, she was almost arrested for illegally importing goods because she had agreed to hide embroidered handkerchiefs and other small accessories in her clothes, in the hope that their resale would increase her employer's profits and, consequently, her own income. Once in Madrid, she was required to work without rest or free time, and the lady who invited her proved to be particularly demanding. This somewhat traumatic experience would have calmed the enthusiasm of many an ambitious young woman, but Jeanne was used to adversity, and thirsted to discover the world. She returned to Spain the following year, for three months, but this time to Barcelona, at the invitation of a more considerate client, Madame Valenti, and with the written assurance that she could break her contract at any time – it was clear that Jeanne had learned her lesson from her misadventures. This stay in Catalonia was her first contact with the light and colours of the Mediterranean, and the pleasant climate in which she worked reinforced a decision that was maturing within her: it was time to set up on her own and spread her wings. However, she would return to Barcelona once more, in 1886, to work with Madame Valenti during the low season. Jeanne kept a strong connection with Spain, and she later opened two boutiques, one in Barcelona and the other in Madrid.

Um dieses Problem zu umgehen, nahm Jeanne 1884 die Einladung einer Spanierin an, den Sommer in Madrid zu verbringen und dort für sie zu arbeiten. Die Spanierin bot ihr dafür ein attraktives Gehalt, denn Hutmacher aus Paris, bekannt für ihre erstklassige Handwerkskunst, waren sehr begehrt. Es mag aus heutiger Sicht naiv wirken, dass sie sich darauf einließ. Immerhin war die erst 17-jährige Jeanne noch nie verreist und sprach nur Französisch. Da sie aber ein sehr neugieriger Mensch war, versuchte sie ihr Glück. Ihre erste Auslandsreise erwies sich aber leider als Desaster. Kaum hatte Jeanne die Grenze überquert, wäre sie fast wegen illegaler Warenimporte festgenommen worden. In der Hoffnung, den Gewinn ihrer neuen Arbeitgeberin und damit auch ihren eigenen Lohn zu steigern, hatte sie sich bereit erklärt, bestickte Taschentücher und kleine Accessoires in ihrer Kleidung zu verstecken. In Madrid angekommen, musste sie pausenlos arbeiten und hatte keinerlei Freizeit, da sich ihre Arbeitgeberin als äußerst anspruchsvoll erwies. Manch andere ehrgeizige junge Frau wäre angesichts eines solchen fast schon traumatischen Erlebnisses wohl eingeknickt, doch Jeanne war an widrige Umstände gewöhnt und sehnte sich danach, mehr von der Welt zu entdecken. So kehrte sie im folgenden Jahr für drei Monate nach Spanien zurück, diesmal nach Barcelona. Ihre dortige Arbeitgeberin, Madame Valenti, war eine weitaus freundlichere Person und Jeanne hatte sich schriftlich zusichern lassen, dass sie jederzeit aus dem Vertrag aussteigen konnte. Sie hatte aus ihrer letzten Erfahrung gelernt. Hier in Katalonien begegneten ihr zum ersten Mal das Licht und die Farben des Mittelmeers. Das angenehme Arbeitsklima war schließlich ausschlaggebend für eine Entscheidung, die schon länger in ihr heranreifte: Es war an der Zeit, die Flügel auszubreiten und sich selbstständig zu machen. 1886 kehrte sie noch einmal nach Barcelona zurück, um während der Sommersaison für Madame Valenti zu arbeiten. Auch noch viele Jahre später fühlte sie sich Spanien eng verbunden, und sollte in dem Land eines Tages zwei Boutiquen eröffnen: eine in Barcelona und eine in Madrid.

At the age of eighteen, while still legally a minor – majority was at twenty-one – Jeanne opened her first workshop in two attic rooms located in a building at rue du Marché Saint-Honoré. She could only rely on some savings, on generous credit granted to her by suppliers, and on her strong determination. She knew that some wealthy patrons would call on her, even if the competition among young milliners was tough, and she didn't give up creating hats and doll clothes so as not to lose completely what had allowed her to take her destiny into her hands. Her ability to sew prompted her to go beyond millinery and design dresses, which constituted her first foray into haute couture. Jeanne was tenacious, and her hard work overcame the obstacles. Four years later, in 1889, as France celebrated the centenary of the French Revolution and Paris was hosting a new Exposition Universelle, she finally opened a milliner's shop at 16 rue Boissy d'Anglas, just off the Faubourg-Saint-Honoré, a stone's throw from the glory that was to come. It took her only four more years to relocate the boutique to 22 rue du Faubourg-Saint-Honoré, right next to the Hermès saddlery at 24, and to gradually take over the complete building that will continue to be associated with the brand from then on, and until today.

Hat decorated with roses,
1913.

Mit Rosen verzierter Hut,
1913.

Hat with feather-like
decorations, 1913.

Hut mit federartigen
Verzierungen, 1913.

Im Alter von 18 Jahren eröffnete Jeanne
ihre erste eigene Werkstatt in zwei
Dachgeschossräumen in der Rue du Marché
Saint-Honoré. Sie war zu dem Zeitpunkt
noch minderjährig, da die Volljährigkeit
damals bei 21 Jahren lag. Alles, was sie
hatte, waren ihre Ersparnisse, großzügige
Kredite ihrer Zulieferer und ihre natürliche
Entschlossenheit. Trotz des unter jungen
Hutmachern herrschenden Wettbewerbs
konnte Jeanne sich darauf verlassen, dass
sich einige wohlhabende Kundinnen an sie
wenden würden. Auch das Fertigen von
Hüten und Kleidern für Puppen, das es ihr
erst ermöglicht hatte, ihr Schicksal selbst
in die Hand zu nehmen, gab sie vorerst noch
nicht auf. Dank ihrer außerordentlichen
Nähfertigkeit wagte sie sich außerdem
bald daran, nicht nur Hüte, sondern
auch Kleider zu entwerfen – ein erster
Vorstoß in Richtung Haute Couture. Jeanne
blieb stets beharrlich und konnte sich,
fleißig wie sie war, über alle Hindernisse
hinwegsetzen. So eröffnete sie im Jahr
1889, als Frankreich den 100. Jahrestag der
Französischen Revolution feierte und Paris
erneut Gastgeber der Weltausstellung war,
ihr eigenes Hutmachergeschäft in der Rue
Boissy d'Anglas Nummer 16 – gleich um
die Ecke von der Rue du Faubourg-Saint-
Honoré, wo sie schon bald zu großem Ruhm
gelangen würde. Es dauerte nur vier Jahre
bis zu ihrem Umzug in die Nummer 22 der
Straße, direkt neben der Hermès-Boutique.
Nach und nach übernahm sie das gesamte
Gebäude, das seitdem und bis heute für die
Marke Lanvin steht.

Top: Summer cloche hat, 1925.

Oben: Topfhut für den Sommer, 1925.

Middle: Bonnet, early 1910s.

Mitte: Haube, frühe 1910er Jahre.

Bottom: Summer hat, 1925.

Unten: Sommerhut, 1925.

Top: Fur felt hat
with ostrich feathers,
around 1913.

Oben: Haarfilzhut mit
Straußenfedern, ca. 1913.

Bottom: Hat, around 1920.

Unten: Hut, ca. 1920.

Summer hat, 1940s.

Sommerhut, 1940er Jahre.

p. 37: Straw turban, 1942.

S. 37: Turban aus Stroh, 1942.

Cobra hat, 1938.

Hutmodell „*Cobra*", 1938.

The years that Jeanne had spent establishing herself as a business owner had distracted her from what was, at the time, an imperative social duty: founding a family. While most of her younger brothers had given her nieces and nephews, Jeanne celebrated her twenty-fifth birthday – the traditional age by which young girls should have been married – without caring too much about finding a match. She was neither unattractive nor stupid, and her business gave her a secure financial footing; she just seemed to value her independence, and she feared she would lose it on the day she married. Besides, her mind was constantly turned to work, even when she went to the Longchamp racetrack to observe the dresses of elegant, upper-class ladies with her young sister and confidante Marie-Alix. It was there that fate placed in her path a young dandy, an aristocrat of Italian origin but devoid of fortune, Emilio di Pietro, born in 1872 in Saint-Petersburg, Russia, to a wealthy father who worked in the champagne trade and a mother who was a florist. The death of the father had deprived the family of the ease they had once enjoyed, and Emilio, despite a refined lifestyle, had to work as an office clerk to support himself, as did his younger brother Mario. Was it his light-hearted, adventurous, and somewhat nonchalant character that immediately attracted Jeanne? Neither the age difference – he was five years younger than she was – nor the poor financial situation of her future husband, nor his reputation as a seducer seemed to make her hesitate. Jeanne married Emilio in a civil ceremony on Thursday the 20th of February 1896, followed two days later by the church wedding, where Jeanne shone alongside her new husband in a glamorous white dress, she had designed herself.

Slightly more than a year later, on August 31 in 1897, Jeanne gave birth to her only child, a daughter. Marguerite Marie Blanche di Pietro, as the child was registered, became Jeanne's main reason for living. Her daughter's happiness and education were to play a central role in her life and would largely determine the evolution of the Lanvin brand in the years to come.

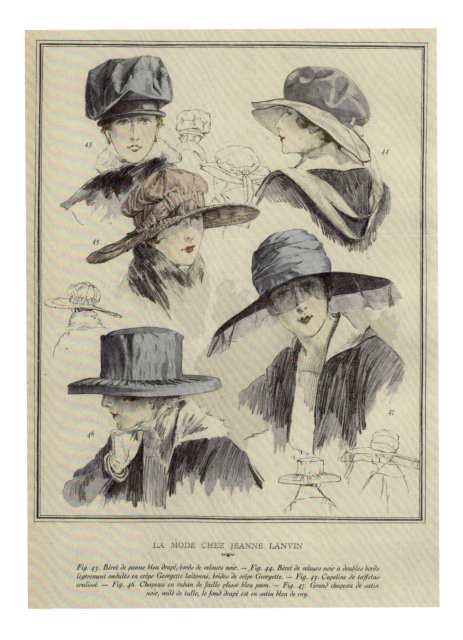

LA MODE CHEZ JEANNE LANVIN

Fig. 43. Béret de panne bleu drapé, bords de velours noir. — Fig. 44. Béret de velours noir à doubles bords légèrement ondulés en crêpe Georgette laitonné, brides de crêpe Georgette. — Fig. 45. Capeline de taffetas coulissé. — Fig. 46. Chapeau en ruban de faille plissé bleu paon. — Fig. 47. Grand chapeau de satin noir, voilé de tulle, le fond drapé est en satin bleu de roy.

Hats by Jeanne Lanvin featured in *Chapeaux des Élégances Parisiennes*, 1917.

Hüte von Jeanne Lanvin in *Chapeaux des Élégances Parisiennes*, 1917.

p. 41: Hat made of velvet petals, 1935.

S. 41: Hut aus Samt-Blütenblättern, 1935.

Da Jeanne sich über Jahre allein auf den Aufbau ihres Geschäfts konzentriert hatte, hatte sie allen gesellschaftlichen Erwartungen zum Trotz keine Familie gegründet. Zwar war sie schon mehrmals Tante geworden, doch ihren 25. Geburtstag – der Zeitpunkt, zu dem junge Frauen traditionell verheiratet sein sollten – feierte sie, ohne sich über einen Ehemann Gedanken zu machen. Sie war weder unattraktiv noch dumm und dank ihres Unternehmens finanziell gut aufgestellt, doch ihre Unabhängigkeit war ihr sehr wichtig und sie befürchtete, diese bei einer Heirat zu verlieren. Außerdem drehten sich ihre Gedanken pausenlos um die Arbeit, selbst wenn sie zum Beispiel mit ihrer Schwester und engen Vertrauten Marie-Alix zum Longchamp-Pferderennen ging, um die eleganten Kleider der Damen aus der Oberschicht zu mustern. Doch wie das Schicksal so spielt, begegnete ihr genau hier ein junger Dandy, ein aus Italien stammender Aristokrat ohne Vermögen namens Emilio di Pietro, der 1872 als Sohn eines wohlhabenden Champagner-Händlers und einer Floristin in St. Petersburg auf die Welt gekommen war. Der Tod des Vaters hatte für die Familie herbe finanzielle Rückschläge bedeutet. Emilio lebte zwar noch ein feines Leben, musste jedoch

ebenso wie sein Bruder Mario in einem Büro arbeiten, um über die Runden zu kommen. War es seine unbeschwerte, abenteuerlustige, nonchalante Art, der Jeanne nicht hatte widerstehen können? Weder der Altersunterschied – Emilio war fünf Jahre jünger als sie – noch seine schlechte finanzielle Lage oder sein Ruf, ein Verführer zu sein, konnten Jeanne von ihrer Entscheidung abbringen. Die standesamtliche Hochzeit von Jeanne und Emilio fand am 20. Februar 1896 statt. Zwei Tage darauf folgte die kirchliche Hochzeit, bei der Jeanne in einem glamourösen weißen Kleid, das sie selbst entworfen hatte, an der Seite ihres neuen Ehemannes strahlte.

Im darauffolgenden Jahr, am 31. August 1897, kam Jeannes einziges Kind, ihre Tochter Marguerite, zur Welt. Marguerite Marie Blanche di Pietro wurde zu Jeannes wichtigster Lebensaufgabe. Ihre Bildung und ihr Glück nahmen eine zentrale Rolle in Jeannes Leben ein und sollten sich maßgeblich auf die weitere Entwicklung der Marke Lanvin auswirken.

Early
Successes

Erste
Erfolge

By the time her daughter Marguerite was born in 1897, Jeanne Lanvin was already a renowned milliner. She had acquired a certain material ease, and her marriage to an Italian count, although he was without fortune, propelled her into the salons of Parisian high society. These exceptional achievements might have satisfied more than one person from a humble social background such as Jeanne's, but for her, everything was still to come. She was certainly not motivated by a desire for social revenge, but rather by her innate curiosity about everything and her business flair, which encouraged her to explore new trends and innovate. At the same time, her entire life seemed to revolve around her daughter Marguerite, whom she lavished with affection. Nothing was too good for the happiness of "Ririte", the little girl's nickname, as if Jeanne wanted to dispel the sadness of her own childhood. She would not let anyone else decide how her daughter should be dressed: all the clothes Marguerite wore were designed and made by Jeanne, with a particular eye to their originality and perfection. Marguerite, who as everyone agreed, had an angelic look, was dressed and hatted like no other child. Whenever other mothers, admiring Marguerite's outfits, would ask Jeanne who her daughter's dressmaker was, she would reply, with natural modesty and simplicity, that it was herself, and would offer to create equally beautiful outfits for their children. Legend has it that in this way, Jeanne Lanvin built up a clientele of loyal customers who entrusted her with the wardrobes of their offspring, and subsequently with their own. Her fame as a talented milliner plus her social connections with the upper class certainly worked in her favour, for in 1901, playwright Edmond Rostand, the author of *Cyrano de Bergerac* and *L'Aiglon*, asked Jeanne Lanvin – to whom he was introduced by the actress Sarah Bernhardt – to tailor and embroider his academician's uniform. Rostand's two most famous plays, written in his twenties, earned him respectively the *Légion d'Honneur*, France's highest distinction – awarded at the premiere of *Cyrano de Bergerac*, in front of an ecstatic audience, by an equally thrilled Minister of Education, and a seat at Académie Française at the age of only 33. Jeanne Lanvin later designed the academician's uniforms for several friends and acquaintances, such as Paul Valéry, André Maurois, François Mauriac, Georges Duhamel, Paul Claudel, and Jean Cocteau, which testified to her links with the French literary and intellectual elite. It was also her first known foray into the world of men's fashion, although the look of the academician's uniform, known in French as the *Habit vert*, was understandably codified.

Meanwhile, in the mid-1900s, women's fashion was undergoing fundamental changes with the abolition of the corset, a quiet revolution initiated by couturiers Madeleine Vionnet and Paul Poiret in 1906, and the comeback of the neoclassical, Empire-style dresses that had been in vogue in the early 19th century. The dresses designed by Jeanne Lanvin in the late 1900s and the early 1910s followed this trend, with a high waist and a long, slim cut. But this more restrained approach to shape was counterbalanced by a deliberate sophistication in the choice of fabrics, embroidery, and selection of colours. This streamlining of the female silhouette led to another evolution that clearly benefited Jeanne Lanvin: what dresses lost in volume, hats took over. Wide-brimmed hats became fashionable, with an exuberance of decoration that was somewhat reminiscent of the fashion for "themed" hairstyles introduced to the court of Versailles by Queen Marie-Antoinette at the end of the 18th century. To keep up with the trends, women inevitably rushed to their milliners to buy the latest hats.

Theaterautor Edmond
Rostand in seiner
Akademie-Uniform, 1903.

Als ihre Tochter Marguerite 1897 auf die Welt kam, war Jeanne Lanvin bereits eine renommierte Hutmacherin. Sie hatte es zu einem gewissen Wohlstand gebracht, und als Ehefrau eines italienischen Grafen – wenn auch ohne Vermögen – hatte sie nun Zugang zu den Salons der gehobenen Gesellschaft. Mit einem solchen Aufstieg wäre so mancher aus ähnlich bescheidenen Verhältnissen mehr als zufrieden gewesen, doch Jeannes Leben war noch zu größeren Erfolgen bestimmt. Der Gedanke, der feinen Gesellschaft etwas beweisen zu müssen, lag ihr allerdings fern. Was sie antrieb, waren vielmehr die Freude an der Arbeit und ihre große Neugier. So blieb sie stets innovativ und zögerte nicht, neue Trends auszuprobieren. Zugleich schien sich in ihrem Leben alles um ihre Tochter zu drehen, die sie mit Zuneigung überschüttete. Für Ririte, wie das kleine Mädchen genannt wurde, war nichts gut genug – fast schon, als wollte Jeanne damit alles verbannen, was an ihre eigene traurige Kindheit erinnern könnte. Niemand außer ihr selbst durfte Marguerite einkleiden. Alle Kleider hatte sie selbst entworfen und genäht und dabei ganz besonders auf Originalität und Perfektion geachtet. Marguerite, die – darin waren sich alle einig – ein engelsgleiches Kind war, war besser gekleidet und behütet als alle anderen Kinder. Wenn andere Mütter Marguerites Kleider bewunderten und fragten, wer sie geschneidert hatte, antwortete Jeanne in ihrer unkomplizierten, bescheidenen Art, dass sie es selbst gewesen war. Sie bot ihnen an, ebenso schöne Kleider für deren Kinder zu fertigen. Der Legende nach gewann Jeanne Lanvin auf diese Weise viele treue Kundinnen, die ihre Kinder und schließlich auch sich selbst von ihr einkleiden ließen. Ihr Ruf als ausgezeichnete Hutmacherin sowie ihre Verbindungen zur Oberschicht kamen ihr dabei zugute. Nachdem sie ihm von Schauspielerin Sarah Bernhardt vorgestellt worden war, ließ der Schriftsteller Edmond Rostand, Autor der Theaterstücke *Cyrano de Bergerac* und *Der junge Adler* seine Akademie-Uniform von Jeanne schneidern und besticken. Für seine berühmtesten Stücke, die er als nicht mal 30-Jähriger geschrieben hatte, erhielt der Dramaturg Frankreichs höchsten Orden, die *Légion d'Honneur*, der ihm bei der Premiere von *Cyrano de Bergerac* vor begeistertem Publikum vom Bildungsminister verliehen wurde. Gleichzeitig sicherte er sich damit einen Platz in der Académie Française – im Alter von nur 33 Jahren. Jeanne entwarf später noch weitere Akademie-Uniformen für Freunde und Bekannte, darunter Paul Valéry, André Maurois, François Mauriac, Georges Duhamel, Paul Claudel und Jean Cocteau. Ihre Verbindungen zur literarischen und intellektuellen Elite Frankreichs waren damit fest etabliert. Zwar gab es bei der Gestaltung der Uniformen, die in Frankreich unter dem Namen *habit vert* bekannt sind, nur wenig Spielraum für Kreativität, dennoch war Jeanne mit deren Fertigung erstmals in die Welt der Herrenmode vorgestoßen.

In der Damenmode kam es um 1906 währenddessen zu einer stillen Revolution, die tiefgreifende Veränderungen nach sich zog: Auf Initiative von Madeleine Vionnet und Paul Poiret, zweier bekannter Modeschöpfer, wurde das Korsett abgeschafft. Angesagt waren jetzt wieder neoklassizistische Kleider im Empire-Stil, wie sie Anfang des 19. Jahrhunderts bereits *en vogue* gewesen waren. Auch die von Jeanne Lanvin in den späten 1900er und frühen 1910er Jahren entworfenen Kleider entsprachen mit länglichen, schmalen Schnitten und hoch angesetzter Taille diesem Trend. Als Ausgleich zu den zurückhaltenden Silhouetten wählte sie für ihre Kreationen bewusst raffinierte Stoffe, Stickereien und Farben. Eine weitere Entwicklung, die Jeanne sehr zugute kam, ergab sich aus den schlichteren Kleiderformen, die nun modern waren: Was die Kleider an Opulenz eingebüßt hatten, verlagerte sich auf den Kopf. *En vogue* waren nun Hüte mit breiter Krempe und üppigen Verzierungen, die an Marie-Antoinettes Haarkreationen im späten 18. Jahrhundert erinnerten. Also strömten Frauen in Scharen zu den Hutmachern, um die neuesten Hutmodelle zu ergattern.

Dresses and accessories
by Jeanne Lanvin,
late 1900s. Photographs
by Paul Nadar.

Kleider und Accessoires
von Jeanne Lanvin,
späte 1900er Jahre.
Fotografien von Paul
Nadar.

Two examples of high-waist dresses popular in the 1900s. Photographs by Paul Nadar.

Zwei Beispiele für die Kleider mit hoch angesetzter Taille, die in den 1900er Jahren modern waren. Fotografien von Paul Nadar.

"Jeanne Lanvin's fashion
is the quintessence
of good taste combined
with modern creativity.
Is it because Madame Lanvin
began by designing clothes
for children? Everything that
comes out of her house
is young, spring-like,
and offers some kind of
airy grace."

*La Renaissance de l'art français
et des industries de luxe, 1924*

Toddler's coat, early 1930s.

Mantel für Kleinkinder, frühe 1930er Jahre.

„Jeanne Lanvins Mode ist guter Geschmack verbunden mit moderner Kreativität. Liegt es daran, dass Madame Lanvin zunächst Kinderkleider entworfen hat? Alles aus ihrem Haus wirkt jung, schwungvoll und auf fast schon schwerelose Art anmutig."

La Renaissance de l'art français et des industries de luxe, 1924

But let us for a moment get back to Marguerite: her early years resembled the imaginary ones that Marcel Proust had invented for Gilberte Swann, the narrator's childhood friend and first love in *In Search of Lost Time*. Like Gilberte, Jeanne Lanvin's daughter played with her comrades in the alleys of the Champs-Elysées gardens, where she often met her future suitors, Georges Gatineau-Clémenceau and René Jacquemaire-Clémenceau, whose grandfather was the powerful Minister of the Interior and President of the Cabinet, Georges Clémenceau. She also made friends with the young Francis Poulenc, who later became a famous composer and one of her confidants. Marguerite received a good education at the Cours Dieterlen, a school for girls from the social elite, where her mother was keen to establish ties with potential clients for her brand. Marguerite also took piano lessons with a young musical prodigy, Lucie Caffaret, who served as an example of diligence for the young Marguerite and helped her develop a passion for music and singing. Her parents' divorce in 1903, when Marguerite was six, did not seem to affect the young girl too much, as she had been constantly surrounded by maternal love. In fact, since the birth of their daughter, the slightly immature Emilio had been an impediment in Jeanne's life and their separation constituted a form of emancipation, even if it went against the conventions of the time and prompted eyebrows to be raised. She took on sole responsibility for Marguerite's education, even though she chose to remarry a few years later – a second marriage that would end equally disastrously, but more on that later.

Doch kehren wir nochmal zurück zu Marguerite. Ihre ersten Lebensjahre erinnern an die Kindheit von Gilberte Swann, Freundin und erste Liebe des Erzählers in Marcel Prousts *Auf der Suche nach der verlorenen Zeit*. Ganz wie Gilberte spielte Jeanne Lanvins Tochter mit ihren Kameraden in den Parks rund um die Champs-Élysées. Hier traf sie regelmäßig ihre künftigen Verehrer Georges Gatineau-Clémenceau und René Jacquemaire-Clémenceau, Enkel des einflussreichen Innenministers und Kabinettsvorsitzenden Georges Clémenceau. Sie freundete sich ebenso mit dem jungen Francis Poulenc an, der später ein berühmter Komponist und einer ihrer engen Vertrauten werden sollte. Marguerite besuchte die *Cours Dieterlen*, eine Schule für Töchter aus wohlhabendem Hause. Ihre Mutter nutzte die Gelegenheit, hier Kontakte zur gesellschaftlichen Elite und somit potenziellen Kunden zu knüpfen. Marguerite nahm Klavierunterricht bei der in der damaligen Musikszene als Wunderkind bekannten Lucie Caffaret, die ihr ein Vorbild war und der sie ihre Leidenschaft für die Musik verdankte. Die Scheidung ihrer Eltern im Jahr 1903, als sie sechs Jahre alt war, schien Marguerite aufgrund der sehr engen Bindung zu ihrer Mutter nicht allzu sehr zu erschüttern. Tatsächlich war der recht unreife Emilio seit der Geburt des Kindes eher ein Hindernis in Jeannes Leben gewesen. Zwar ging die Trennung gegen alle zeitgenössischen Konventionen und erntete den ein oder anderen missbilligenden Blick, doch für Jeanne war sie ein emanzipatorischer Akt. Sie übernahm die alleinige Verantwortung für Marguerites Erziehung und heiratete einige Jahre später erneut – eine zweite Ehe, die ebenso desaströs endete wie die erste, doch dazu später mehr.

Marguerite, Jeanne Lanvin's daughter, with a model, photographed by Paul Nadar, 1900s.

Jeanne Lanvins Tochter Marguerite mit einem Modell, von Paul Nadar fotografiert, 1900er Jahre.

The never-ending fittings for new clothes that Jeanne imposed on her daughter were arguably Marguerite's only annoyance, for she became her mother's favourite fashion model, and was given a promotional mission against her will. Jeanne Lanvin, with her keen intelligence and visionary spirit, decided in 1908 to innovate by creating a department dedicated to children's clothing. Instead of designing children's outfits that would imitate those of their parents and turn the little ones into miniature adults, Jeanne Lanvin wanted to create clothes that would be more suited to the anatomy of young children and their activities; outfits in cheerful colours, with fabrics that were soft to the touch and comfortable to wear, and with more original decorative patterns than those for grown-ups. Her experience manufacturing doll clothes and hats as an additional income during her apprenticeship years undoubtedly fuelled her inspiration: indeed, many of the children's clothes seemed to come from a dream-like, imaginary world, as if they had escaped from a fairy tale. It might seem paradoxical that this naturally shy, self-effacing, and modest mother would do everything to ensure that her daughter, on the contrary, would attract all the attention. Only a peerless maternal pride, and the desire to see her daughter enjoy an enchanted early life might explain this rather unexpected behaviour.

Die ständigen Kleideranproben, die Marguerite über sich ergehen lassen musste, waren vermutlich das größte Ärgernis ihrer Jugend. Sie war das Lieblingsmodell ihrer Mutter und wurde gegen ihren Willen als Werbebotschafterin eingesetzt. Intelligent und vorausschauend wie sie war, beschloss Jeanne Lanvin 1908 eine Abteilung nur für Kinderkleidung ins Leben zu rufen. Statt wie damals üblich Kinderkleidung zu entwerfen, in der die Kleinen wie Erwachsene im Miniaturformat aussahen, wollte Jeanne Lanvin ihre Kleidung an den Körperbau und die Aktivitäten von Kindern anpassen. So entstanden farbenfrohe, bequeme Kleider aus angenehm weichen Stoffen, die mit originelleren Mustern geziert wurden als die der Erwachsenen. Die Erfahrung, die sie während ihrer Lehrjahre beim Fertigen von Puppenkleidern und -hüten gesammelt hatte, beflügelte dabei ohne Zweifel ihre Fantasie. Viele der Kinderkleider schienen einer märchenhaften Traumwelt zu entstammen. Auf den ersten Blick mag es widersprüchlich erscheinen, dass eine so schüchterne, bescheidene Person alles dafür tat, dass ihre Tochter stets im Mittelpunkt stand. Vermutlich waren es ihr mütterlicher Stolz und ihr Wunsch, ihrer Tochter ein wahrhaft bezauberndes Leben zu ermöglichen.

Without renouncing her activity as a milliner, Jeanne Lanvin joined the *Syndicat de la Couture* (Couturiers' Guild) in 1909, thus formalising her new activity. As Marguerite was growing into adolescence, the ever-caring mother expanded her business to open a teenage department, and another for ladies. She would soon add two more departments, one devoted to wedding dresses – an activity that seemed to be close to her heart and that she would develop in the decades to come – and the other dedicated to furs, thus gradually completing the range of clothing that the brand was able to offer its luxury-oriented clientele. In the midst of this incessant activity, Jeanne Lanvin found time in 1907 to marry a former journalist turned diplomat, Xavier Mélet. His position as French vice-consul in Manchester, England, which looked like a middle-ranking sinecure, offered him enough free time to travel with his wife to the French Riviera and Italy, where he introduced her to the world of art and museums. Tired of the British fogs, Mélet resigned his post in 1908 to enjoy a leisurely life in one of the villas his wife had acquired in the south of France. While Jeanne was pleased to have regained some form of social standing through this marriage – her status as a divorced woman and single mother was certainly not enviable – she soon grew weary of this somewhat pretentious freeloader. By the time of Mélet's death in 1953, seven years after Jeanne's, he had been almost forgotten by the Lanvin family, as there was no longer any link between them, nevertheless Mélet was buried in the same family vault at Le Vésinet, near Paris.

Ohne die Hutmacherei aufzugeben, trat Jeanne 1909 dem Verband der Modeschöpfer (*Syndicat de la Couture*) bei, wodurch ihre neue Tätigkeit offiziell wurde. Während Marguerite langsam erwachsen wurde, lancierte Jeanne eine eigene Abteilung mit Mode für Jugendliche und eine weitere für Damenmode. Bald sollten zwei weitere Sparten dazukommen: eine für Brautkleider – ein Thema, das ihr sehr am Herzen lag – und eine für Pelzwaren – womit das Angebot im Luxussegment nach und nach vervollständigt wurde. Zu den zahlreichen beruflichen Entwicklungen kam 1907 Jeannes zweite Hochzeit mit dem ehemaligen Journalisten Xavier Mélet, der inzwischen als Diplomat tätig war. Seine wenig anspruchsvolle Anstellung als französischer Vize-Konsul im englischen Manchester ließ ihm genug Freizeit, um mit seiner Frau an die französische Riviera und nach Italien zu reisen, wo er sie in die Welt der Kunst und Museen einführte. Als er dem englischen Nebel überdrüssig war, gab Mélet seinen Posten 1908 auf, um das Leben in einer Villa in Südfrankreich zu genießen, die seine Frau zuvor erstanden hatte. Zwar war Jeanne, deren Status als geschiedene Frau und alleinerziehende Mutter geschwächt war, froh, durch diese Heirat wieder mehr gesellschaftliches Ansehen zu genießen, doch sie hatte von dem recht hochnäsigen Trittbrettfahrer Mélet schnell genug. Als Mélet 1953 sieben Jahre nach Jeanne starb, war er von ihrer Familie fast schon vergessen worden, da sie kaum noch miteinander zu tun gehabt hatten. Dennoch wurde Mélet im Lanvin-Familiengrab in Le Vésinet in der Nähe von Paris bestattet.

pp. 62-63: Marguerite with dresses and hats designed by her mother Jeanne, 1900s.

S. 62-63: Marguerite in Kleidern und Hüten ihrer Mutter Jeanne, 1900er Jahre.

Winter fashion, 1909. Photography by Paul Nadar.

Wintermode, 1909. Fotografie von Paul Nadar.

Evening dress,
1909, with detail of
the embroidered sleeve.

Abendkleid, 1909,
mit Detailansicht
des bestickten Ärmels.

Wedding dresses in Jeanne Lanvin's œuvre

In the Belle Époque, marriage was an unshakeable institution of social life. The wedding ceremony was not simply a rite of passage to full adult status, but also an opportunity to seal social, financial, business, or even diplomatic alliances between families, as exemplified by the royal and princely houses whose dynastic ties were regularly strengthened by marriages between members of reigning families. Although it might only be worn on one day, the wedding dress had to reflect the solemnity of the celebration, and it was then treasured as a lifelong souvenir. White, a colour rarely worn alone in everyday life, had been mainly perceived as a symbol of purity since the Renaissance, and was de rigueur for the wedding dress. All other elements of the dress were left to the discretion of the bride-to-be and her parents, but the general opinion was that it ought to be a unique piece arousing unanimous admiration and shining with splendour. From the creation of the wedding dresses department onwards, Jeanne Lanvin would employ all her creative talent at the service of future brides, constantly inventing new embroidery motifs and tirelessly switching from classic cuts to models that were more in tune with the fashion of the moment.

Her knowledge of historical costume and her exceptional visual memory allowed her to draw inspiration from dresses of the past centuries or models from other cultures – notably Spanish or Russian, as the Russian ballets, which premiered in Paris in 1909, sparked a craze for the aesthetics of the Tsarist Empire. Her expertise in the field of children's and teenage clothing also inspired her to create dresses for bridesmaids, as can be seen in fashion illustrations and some photographs. One can easily imagine the joy she must have felt in 1917 when she designed the wedding dress for her own daughter Marguerite, who married her childhood sweetheart, surgeon René Jacquemaire-Clémenceau. In photos showing the young couple on their wedding day, the sober uniform of the groom – he was still mobilised – brought out even more the magnificence of the dress on which the mother has embroidered with a huge daisy ("marguerite", in French).

Wedding dress, fashion illustration, 1924.

Brautkleid, Modeillustration, 1924.

p. 69: Wedding dress, fashion illustration, 1921.

S. 69: Brautkleid, Modeillustration, 1921.

Brautkleider
von Jeanne Lanvin

Zur Zeit der Belle Époque war die Ehe ein unantastbarer Bestandteil gesellschaftlichen Lebens. Die Eheschließung war nicht nur der endgültige Schritt ins Erwachsensein, sondern auch eine Gelegenheit, soziale, finanzielle, geschäftliche oder gar diplomatische Beziehungen zwischen zwei Familien aufzubauen. Das beste Beispiel dafür sind bekanntlich die Fürsten- und Königshäuser, die ihre Machtansprüche häufig durch Eheschließungen zwischen Mitgliedern der herrschenden Familien untermauerten. Obwohl es nur ein einziges Mal getragen wurde, fiel dem Hochzeitskleid dabei

eine große Bedeutung zu. Es musste dem feierlichen Anlass gewachsen sein und wurde anschließend als wertvolles Erinnerungsstück aufbewahrt. Die Farbe Weiß, ein Muss für das Brautkleid, wurde im Alltag nur selten getragen. Bereits seit der Renaissance galt Weiß als Symbol der Reinheit. Wie das Brautkleid darüber hinaus aussah, wurde von der zukünftigen Braut und ihren Eltern entschieden. Originell sollte es sein – und zahlreiche bewundernde Blicke auf sich ziehen. Mit der Gründung der Brautkleidabteilung schenkte Jeanne Lanvin ihre kreative Energie den zukünftigen Bräuten. Ständig entwarf sie neue Stickmotive und bot sowohl traditionell geschnittene Kleider als auch Modelle an, die die aktuelle Mode widerspiegelten. Dank ihrer modegeschichtlichen Kenntnisse und ihres ausgezeichneten visuellen Gedächtnisses konnte sie sich von Kleidern vergangener Jahrhunderte oder aus anderen Kulturen inspirieren lassen. Insbesondere spanische und russische Einflüsse spielten dabei eine große Rolle. Das russische Ballett, das in Paris 1909 zum ersten Mal aufgeführt worden war, löste eine Welle der Begeisterung für die Ästhetik des Zarenreiches aus. Ihre Arbeit in der Kinder- und Jugendmode inspirierte sie dazu, auch Kleider für Brautjungfern zu entwerfen, wie in zeitgenössischen Illustrationen und auf einigen Fotos zu sehen ist. Welch großes Glück sie empfunden haben musste, als sie das Brautkleid ihrer Tochter entwarf, als diese ihre große Liebe aus Kindheitstagen, den Chirurgen René Jacquemaire-Clémenceau, heiratete. Auf den Hochzeitsfotos sieht man den Bräutigam, der zum Militär eingezogen worden war, in seiner nüchternen Uniform. Daneben strahlt die Braut umso schöner. In Anlehnung an ihren Namen hatte ihre Mutter eine riesige Margerite auf das Kleid gestickt.

p. 70: Wedding dress,
fashion illustration,
around 1912.

S. 70: Brautkleid,
Modeillustration,
ca. 1912.

Wedding ensemble,
1925.

Brautkleid mit
Accessoires, 1925.

1910-1919

The Rising Star
of Haute Couture

Der aufstrebende Star
der Haute Couture

In the light of what would be her future successes, Jeanne Lanvin's rise in the world of haute couture in the early 1910s had seemed assured. However, despite her undoubted talent, nothing was guaranteed, for luxury couture was still an all-male domain: at the beginning of the 20th century, men's domination over women's fashion was still unchallenged. Although Charles-Frederick Worth had died in 1895, considered the founder of modern haute couture and the supreme authority on elegance during the Third Empire, his sons Jean-Philippe and Gaston had taken over the reins and perpetuated the tradition. Another great name in women's fashion of the Belle Epoque, Jacques Doucet, boasted among his clients renowned actresses of the time such as Réjane and Sarah Bernhardt, as well as the Countess Elisabeth Greffuhle, a patron and muse of many artists – she inspired Proust's character of the Duchess de Guermantes. Despite the aura of prestige surrounding the houses of Worth and Doucet at the turn of the century, along with their peers Paquin and Redfern, their domination of Parisian fashion would be challenged in 1903 by Paul Poiret, a young designer who had, interestingly, trained with both. Like no other designer, Poiret embodied the spirit of the Belle Époque: it can be said, to borrow the French title of his autobiography, that he was dressing his time. He was also a great seducer, in his autobiography he recounted some of his affairs with famous actresses. While Jeanne Lanvin was modest, self-effacing, and prudent in business, Poiret was exuberant, extravagant, and profligate, yet his example and work provided lasting inspiration for a new generation of couturiers to which Jeanne belonged. He was in some respects the first stylist in the modern sense of the word, for he did not regard his activity as a craft, but rather as artistic creation – in fact, he had begun his career at Doucet as an illustrator. Poiret played a significant role in the abolition of the corset in the first decade of the 20th century, and in the reintroduction of the Empire-style dress, with its high waist and straight lines that gave the woman a much more natural look.

He brought bright and joyful colours back into fashion, as opposed to the pastel and muted shades that had prevailed during the 19th century. Drawing inspiration from the splendour of oriental costumes, Poiret designed sumptuously exotic, somewhat eccentric garments, such as caftans, baggy trousers, and ornate kimonos. He was the first couturier to launch a range of perfumes in 1911, well before Jeanne Lanvin and Coco Chanel, and created around forty of them during his career. Above all, he contributed to the success of a fashion magazine that became the benchmark of Parisian elegance, the *Gazette du Bon Ton*, whose first issue was published in November 1912. Its fashion plates were created by the best illustrators of the time, such as Paul Iribe, Georges Lepape and even Léon Bakst, who had become famous thanks to his sumptuous decorations for the Ballets Russes. Jeanne Lanvin began to show her designs in the magazine from March 1914, which marked her recognition as one of the most prominent couturiers of the time, following the Grand Prix she received in 1913 for the dresses she exhibited at the Exposition Universelle in Ghent, Belgium.

p. 72: Afternoon dress, around 1912.

S. 72: Gesellschaftskleid, ca. 1912.

Paul Poiret, an avant-garde fashion designer and a long-time friend of Jeanne Lanvin.

Paul Poiret, avantgardistischer Modeschöpfer und langjähriger Freund Jeanne Lanvins.

p. 75: The Lanvin headquarters at 22 rue du Faubourg-Saint-Honoré, Paris in the 1910s.

S. 75: Das Lanvin-Hauptquartier in der Rue du Faubourg Saint-Honoré Nummer 22 in Paris in den 1910er Jahren.

Denkt man an den Riesenerfolg, den Jeanne Lanvin noch erleben würde, scheint ihr Aufstieg in die Haute Couture in den 1910er Jahren unvermeidlich. Doch trotz ihres unbestrittenen Talents war der Aufstieg kein Selbstläufer – denn die Welt der Luxusmode wurde ganz klar von Männern beherrscht. Dass die Männer am Anfang des 20. Jahrhunderts auch in der Damenmode das Sagen hatten, war eine unangefochtene Selbstverständlichkeit. Nachdem Charles-Frederick Worth, der als Gründer der modernen Haute Couture und wichtigste Instanz eleganter Mode in der dritten Republik gilt, 1895 gestorben war, nahmen seine Söhne Jean-Philippe und Gaston das Zepter in die Hand und führten die Tradition damit fort. Eine weitere Schlüsselfigur der Damenmode der Belle Époque war Jacques Doucet, zu dessen Kundinnen berühmte Schauspielerinnen wie Réjane und Sarah Bernhardt sowie Gräfin Elisabeth Greffulhe gehörten. Die Gräfin war Förderin und Muse vieler Künstler. So hatte sich Proust für die Figur der Herzogin von Guermantes von ihr inspirieren lassen. Trotz des großen Prestiges der Modehäuser Worth und Doucet wie auch Paquin und Redfern, wurde ihre Dominanz im Jahr 1903 durch den jungen Modeschöpfer Paul Poiret herausgefordert, der interessanterweise sowohl von Worth als auch von Doucet ausgebildet worden war. Paul Poiret verkörperte den Zeitgeist der Belle Époque wie kein anderer. Wie der Titel seiner Autobiografie *En habillant l'époque* vermuten lässt, war er es, der die Belle Époque einkleidete. Poiret war als großer Verführer bekannt und erzählt in seiner Autobiografie von zahlreichen Affären mit berühmten Schauspielerinnen. Seine Persönlichkeit war das Gegenteil von Jeanne Lanvins bescheidener, zurückhaltender Art und ihren vorausschauenden unternehmerischen Entscheidungen. Poiret war überschwänglich, extravagant und verschwenderisch, seine Arbeit jedoch

war Vorbild und Inspiration für eine gesamte Generation neuer Modeschöpfer, zu der auch Jeanne gehörte. In gewisser Hinsicht war er der erste Designer im heutigen Sinne – seine Arbeit sah er nicht als Handwerk, sondern als künstlerisches Schaffen. So hatte er seine Karriere bei Doucet auch als Modezeichner begonnen. Poiret spielte bei der Abschaffung des Korsetts in den 1910er Jahren eine wichtige Rolle und trug maßgeblich zur Wiederkehr des Empire-Kleides bei, das durch die hoch angesetzte Taille und gerade Linienführung die natürlichen weiblichen Formen zum Ausdruck brachte. Dank seiner Entwürfe hielten kräftige, lebhafte Farben wieder Einzug in die Mode – ein deutlicher Kontrast zu den gedeckten Farben und Pastelltönen, die im 19. Jahrhundert so dominant waren. Poiret ließ sich von der Pracht orientalischer Trachten inspirieren und entwarf herrlich exotische, fast schon exzentrische Kleidungsstücke wie Kaftane, Hosen mit weitem Bein und reich verzierte Kimonos. 1911 brachte er als erster Modeschöpfer eine Parfumlinie auf den Markt – lange bevor Jeanne Lanvin und Coco Chanel es ihm gleichtaten. Insgesamt brachte er im Laufe seiner Karriere rund 40 Parfums heraus. Ganz besonders trug er auch zum Erfolg der Zeitschrift *Gazette du Bon Ton* bei, die 1912 erstmals erschien und bald zum Maßstab für elegante Pariser Mode wurde. Die darin enthaltenen Illustrationen stammten von den besten Illustratoren der damaligen Zeit, darunter Paul Iribe, Georges Lepape und Léon Bakst, der mit seinen ausgefallenen Kostümen für das *Ensemble Ballets Russes* berühmt wurde. Nachdem Jeanne Lanvin 1913 für ihre Kleider bei der Weltausstellung in Gent einen Grand Prix erhalten hatte, wurden ihre Entwürfe ab März 1914 auch in der *Gazette du Bon Ton* gezeigt – ein Hinweis auf ihre Anerkennung als eine der bedeutendsten Modeschöpferinnen ihrer Zeit.

THE RISING STAR OF HAUTE COUTURE / DER AUFSTREBENDE STAR DER HAUTE COUTURE (1910-1919)

p. 78: Embroidered afternoon dress, 1913.

Fashion illustration, mid-1910s.

S. 78: Besticktes Gesellschaftskleid, 1913.

Modeillustration, Mitte der 1910er Jahre.

Although Jeanne Lanvin adhered to Poiret's stylistic innovations and shared his passion for colour, she nevertheless showed a certain originality in her sources of inspiration, which were much more diverse than those of her peer. They included Renaissance and Baroque fashions, Spanish and Italian elements, Middle- and Far Eastern traditions, which she freely reinterpreted with the sole desire of satisfying an ever-growing clientele, who undoubtedly appreciated her simplicity, knowledge, and love of detail. Her personality was the antithesis of an ego such as that of Poiret who had prided himself for turning away the Baroness Henri de Rothschild because she had ridiculed one of his collections. Truth be told, Poiret seemed to have earned the Baron's sympathy by doing so, as the latter could call on the couturier with his mistress without fearing to meet his wife there. Like in Aesop's fable about the hare and the tortoise, while Poiret threw enchanting parties in his private mansion at Faubourg-Saint-Honoré attracting the Parisian elite who marvelled at the pomp and circumstance, and while his travels throughout Europe, as far as Saint Petersburg, won him the favour of the European courts – he visited the family of the German Emperor Wilhelm II in Potsdam a few weeks before the outbreak of the First World War – Jeanne Lanvin kept on moving forward at her own, safe pace. The choice of fabrics and the refined embroidery that characterised her dresses and coats in the early 1910s were in line with the expert work that she had already accomplished as a milliner. Although fashion plates were at their height of popularity in the early 1910s, she turned to a relatively new medium, photography, and retained the services of Paul Nadar, the son of Félix Nadar the famous portrait photographer and pioneer of aerial photography, to document her collections. The advantage of Nadar's photographs was that they made the extreme elegance of the dresses and accessories tangible and alive, as opposed to the fashion plates that tended to place the models in the context of idealised social interactions.

p. 80: Silk coat,
around 1913.

S. 80: Seidenmantel,
ca. 1913.

Russian-style blouse,
around 1912

Bluse im russischen Stil,
ca. 1912.

Zwar richtete sich Jeanne Lanvin durchaus nach Poirets stilistischen Neuerungen und teilte seine Vorliebe für kräftige Farben, doch ihre Kreationen waren stets einzigartig. Ihre Originalität zeigte, dass ihre Inspirationsquellen einfach vielfältiger als die ihrer Kollegen waren. Die Mode der Renaissance und des Barock, spanische und italienische Einflüsse, Elemente aus traditioneller Kleidung des Nahen und Fernen Ostens – all das wurde von ihr ganz frei auf neue Weise interpretiert. Ihre ständig wachsende Kundschaft schätzte sie dafür – genauso wie für ihre unkomplizierte Art, ihr großes Wissen und ihre Liebe zum Detail. Charakterlich war sie der klare Gegenentwurf zu Poiret mit seinem großen Ego. Er prahlte sogar damit, die Baronin Rothschild als Kundin abgewiesen zu haben, nachdem sie sich über eine seiner Kollektionen lustig gemacht hatte. Tatsächlich hatte er sich damit bei Baron Rothschild beliebt gemacht – dieser konnte den Modeschöpfer mit seiner Geliebten besuchen, ohne Angst haben zu müssen, dort auf seine Frau zu stoßen. Das Verhältnis zwischen Jeanne Lanvin und Poiret erinnert ein bisschen an den Hasen und die Schildkröte aus Äsops Fabel. Poiret gab in seiner Stadtvilla ausschweifende Feste, bei denen er die Pariser Elite mit Glanz und Gloria begeisterte. Er reiste durch ganz Europa bis nach St. Petersburg und gewann damit die europäischen Höfe für sich. Wenige Wochen vor dem Ausbruch des ersten Weltkriegs besuchte er sogar die Familie von Kaiser Wilhelm II in Potsdam. Währenddessen entwickelte sich Jeanne Lanvin in ihrem eigenen Tempo beständig weiter. Die feinen Stoffe und raffinierten Stickereien, die ihre Kleider und Mäntel in den frühen 1910er Jahren ausmachten, standen der Qualität ihrer Hutmacherarbeit in nichts nach. Obwohl Modeillustrationen in den frühen 1910er Jahren am Höhepunkt ihrer Beliebtheit waren, wandte sie sich dem relativ neuen Medium der Fotografie zu. Dafür nahm sie die Dienste von Paul Nadar, Sohn des berühmten Porträtfotografen und Pioniers der Luftfotografie Félix Nadar in Anspruch, um ihre Kollektionen zu präsentieren. Nadars Fotografien hatten den Vorteil, die Kleider und Accessoires lebhaft und realistisch darzustellen, so dass deren Eleganz perfekt zum Ausdruck kam – anders als in den Modeillustrationen, in denen die Modelle idealisiert präsentiert wurden.

Afternoon dress, 1913,
with details of
the embroidery.

Gesellschaftskleid, 1913,
mit Detailansicht
der Verzierungen.

THE RISING STAR OF HAUTE COUTURE / DER AUFSTREBENDE STAR DER HAUTE COUTURE (1910-1919)

THE RISING STAR OF HAUTE COUTURE / DER AUFSTREBENDE STAR DER HAUTE COUTURE (1910-1919)

p. 84: Various winter dresses and hats, early 1910s.
Photographs by Paul Nadar.

S. 84: Verschiedene Hüte und Kleider für den Winter,
frühe 1910er Jahre. Fotografien von Paul Nadar.

Assorted hat and dress with grapes
and wine leaves, early 1910s

Hut und Kleid mit Trauben-
und Weinblattmotiven, frühe 1910er Jahre.

Empire-style dress with a fur collar, early 1910s.

Empire-Kleid mit Pelzkragen, frühe 1910er Jahre.

Oriental dress inspired by the Russian ballets in Paris, early 1910s.

Orientalisch anmutendes Kleid, vom russischen Ballett in Paris inspiriert, frühe 1910er Jahre.

THE RISING STAR OF HAUTE COUTURE / DER AUFSTREBENDE STAR DER HAUTE COUTURE (1910-1919)

THE RISING STAR OF HAUTE COUTURE / DER AUFSTREBENDE STAR DER HAUTE COUTURE (1910-1919)

A decade that looked set to be prosperous and innovative, not only in fashion but also in the worlds of culture and science, suddenly descended into the horror of war in the summer of 1914. At the beginning of the conflict, however, optimism prevailed, and a wave of patriotism swept through each of the belligerent countries as none doubted that a swift victory would be possible. Poiret, at age 35, was mobilised, like many men of his age, and closed his fashion house for an indefinite period that, he hoped, would be as short as possible. Male employees of the Lanvin house and some of Jeanne's brothers were called up for military duty, but as haute couture predominantly employed female staff and there was no reason for the business to stop. The first restrictions were felt quite quickly when spinning mills in the north of France were cut off from the rest of the country by the front line, and Jeanne Lanvin chose to replace some fabrics made of wool and cottons with silks from Lyon, particularly in the children's collections. As a far-sighted businesswoman, she had anticipated the fall in domestic demand and was looking for new clientele outside Europe, in addition to the Argentine market that she had already conquered. What event could be timelier than the San Francisco World's Fair, which opened in February 1915 and attracted nearly twenty million visitors? San Francisco was, in the eyes of Europeans of the time, the end of the civilized world, but this did not deter Jeanne Lanvin.

The French haute couture delegation received a triumphal welcome. The French pavilion, a replica of the Palais de la Légion d'Honneur in Paris, was built with the financial support of a Francophile American millionaire and provided a magnificent setting for the collections on show. The participation of French haute couture brands in the Panama-Pacific International Exposition, as the World's Fair in San Francisco was officially called, reflected the efforts of the Syndicate for the Defence of French Haute Couture, founded in 1914 on the initiative of Paul Poiret, to counter the practice of cheap counterfeiting that was widespread in the United States at the time, and damaged the reputation of French luxury fashion. By exhibiting collections from the best Parisian haute couture houses, the Syndicate hoped to convince the American public that French fashion designs offered unrivalled quality and sophistication. On the way back to France, a party in honour of French haute couture was held at the Ritz-Carlton in New York in November 1915, which confirmed the enthusiasm of American high society for French fashion. By the end of the war, the United States had become the second largest export market for French haute couture after the United Kingdom, and Poiret, ever the forerunner, had opened a boutique in New York by 1917.

p. 88: Afternoon dress, early 1910s.

S. 88: Gesellschaftskleid, frühe 1910er Jahre.

p. 89: Summer coat, headband, and dress, early 1910s.

S. 89: Leichter Mantel, Stirnband und Kleid, frühe 1910er Jahre.

p. 90: Hat and summer dress with decorative ribbon, early 1910s.

S. 90: Hut und Sommerkleid mit Zierbändern, frühe 1910er Jahre.

p. 91: Large-brimmed hat, dress, and muff, early 1910s.

S. 91: Breitkrempiger Hut, Kleid und Muff, frühe 1910er Jahre.

Some of the dresses featured at *Fête Parisienne*, New York, 1915.

Einige der bei der *Fête Parisienne* gezeigten Kleider, New York, 1915.

CHÉRUIT *(Fig. 274)*.   LANVIN *(Fig. 275)*.   CHÉRUIT *(Fig. 276)*.

LA "FÊTE PARISIENNE" A NEW-YORK

Afternoon dress and
hat, 1916.

Gesellschaftskleid
mit Hut, 1916.

Die weitere Entwicklung des Jahrzehnts, das anfangs nicht nur in der Mode, sondern auch in der Kultur und Wissenschaft von Innovation und Wohlstand geprägt war, nahm mit dem Ausbruch des Krieges 1914 eine unheilvolle Wendung. Zu Beginn des Konflikts gaben sich alle Kriegsparteien optimistisch und wurden von patriotischem Eifer erfasst. Niemand zweifelte daran, dass ein schneller Sieg in Sicht war. Der 35-jährige Paul Poiret wurde wie viele Männer in seinem Alter eingezogen. Er schloss seine Boutique auf unbestimmte Zeit – in der Hoffnung, sie bald wieder öffnen zu können. Männliche Lanvin-Angestellte und einige Brüder von Jeanne wurden ebenfalls eingezogen. Da in der Haute Couture jedoch vorwiegend Frauen arbeiteten, gab es zunächst keinen Grund, das Geschäft einzustellen. Trotzdem waren die ersten Einschränkungen bald spürbar, als etwa die Spinnereien in Nordfrankreich durch den Verlauf der Front vom Rest des Landes abgeschnitten wurden. Jeanne Lanvin ersetzte daher einige Stoffe aus Wolle und Baumwolle, vor allem in den Kinderkollektionen, durch Seide aus Lyon. Als vorausschauende Geschäftsfrau hatte sie mit dem Rückgang der Nachfrage gerechnet und sah sich nun außerhalb Europas nach neuer Kundschaft um. Den argentinischen Markt hatte sie bereits erobert. Die Weltausstellung in San Francisco, die im Februar 1915 öffnete und fast 20 Millionen Besucher anzog, war dafür die perfekte Gelegenheit.

Aus damaliger europäischer Sicht stellte San Francisco das Ende der zivilisierten Welt dar, doch das hielt Jeanne nicht ab. Die französische Haute-Couture-Delegation wurde mit allem Brimborium empfangen. Der französische Pavillon, eine Nachbildung des Pariser Palais de la Légion d'Honneur, wurde von einem amerikanischen Millionär mit einer Schwäche für Frankreich finanziert und erwies sich als großartiger Rahmen für die gezeigten Kollektionen. In den USA waren zur damaligen Zeit viele billige Fälschungen im Umlauf, die dem Ruf französischer Luxusmode geschadet hatten. Um dagegen vorzugehen, war 1914 auf Paul Poirets Initiative hin das Syndikat zur Verteidigung französischer Haute Couture gegründet worden. Die Teilnahme französischer Haute-Couture-Marken an der Weltausstellung war Teil der Strategie des Syndikats. Die feinen Pariser Haute-Couture-Kollektionen sollten die Amerikaner überzeugen, dass die Raffinesse und Qualität französischer Mode einzigartig war. Auf der Rückreise nach Frankreich fand im November 1915 im New Yorker Ritz-Carlton eine Feier zu Ehren der französischen Haute Couture statt, die die Begeisterung der amerikanischen High Society für französische Mode zum Ausdruck brachte. Am Ende des Krieges waren die USA nach Großbritannien der zweitgrößte Exportmarkt für französische Haute Couture. Der ewige Vorreiter Poiret eröffnete bereits 1917 eine Boutique in New York.

In Paris, the war and the increasing loss of human lives led to a new need for mourning dresses, which Jeanne Lanvin undertook to fulfil. While she had always favoured brighter colours, Jeanne Lanvin adopted and adapted all shades of black for the war widows, matching it sometimes with white ornaments. In the same patriotic spirit, she launched garments in blue, white and red. Inspired, like other couturiers of the time, by military and hospital uniforms, she also created the first ladies' suits. Her main innovation there was that the jackets were fitted with pockets, a practical element that had never been used in women's haute couture. Their introduction denoted a trend towards more practical fashion, as women began playing a more active role in society. Meanwhile, to reach a part of her clientele who had withdrawn to fashionable seaside resorts, far from the hostilities, she opened her first two boutiques in Deauville and Biarritz, in the early days of 1916.

1917 was the year of decisive changes and global shifts: while the United States entered the war on the side of the Allies, the Russian Empire, shaken by a chaos that heralded revolution and civil war, pitifully withdrew from the conflict. Few people were aware that this would lead to the loss of an important clientele: the Russian aristocracy and the wealthy industrial bourgeoisie who were particular advocates of French fashion. However, as far as Jeanne Lanvin and her daughter were concerned, 1917 saw the fulfilment of a dream. On 21 May, Marguerite finally married her childhood love, René Jacquemaire-Clémenceau, after three years of waiting, because René, a student of medicine, had been called to the front in 1914. The presence among the guests of Georges Clémenceau, the groom's grandfather and the most popular French politician of the time – he was about to be appointed President of the Cabinet again – showed, if it were necessary, the impressive social rise achieved by Jeanne Lanvin in the thirty years since she set up on her own. And her most successful years were still ahead of her.

p. 96: Embroidered black
silk and organdy dress,
1919.

S. 96: Schwarzes,
besticktes Kleid aus Seide
und Organdy, 1919.

Evening coat, hat,
and gloves, 1917.

Abendmantel, Hut
und Handschuhe, 1917.

Fashion illustrations showing
women's suits by Jeanne Lanvin,
early 1910s.

Modeillustrationen von Jeanne
Lanvins Damenkostümen, frühe
1910er Jahre.

p. 99: Jeanne Lanvin and her
daughter Marguerite, 1913.
Figurine by Lafitte-Désirat.

S. 99: Jeanne Lanvin und ihre
Tochter Marguerite, 1913.
Figur von Lafitte-Désirat.

In Paris hatten die kriegsbedingten Todesfälle zu einer erhöhten Nachfrage nach Trauerkleidern geführt, der Jeanne Lanvin umgehend nachkam. Obwohl sie stets gern kräftige Farben eingesetzt hatte, arbeitete Jeanne Lanvin für die Kleider der Kriegswitwen mit verschiedenen Schwarzschattierungen und verzierte sie hin und wieder mit weißen Ornamenten. Im Sinne des Patriotismus brachte sie außerdem Kleidung in blau, weiß und rot auf den Markt. Wie andere zeitgenössische Modeschaffende ließ sie sich von den Uniformen des Militärs und der Arbeitskleidung des Krankenhauspersonals inspirieren. So entstanden Lanvins erste Anzüge für Damen. Deren große Innovation bestand darin, dass die Jacken über Taschen verfügten. Ein so praktisches Element hatte es in der luxuriösen Damenmode bis dahin nicht gegeben. Diese Neuerung war Ausdruck eines breiteren Trends hin zu praktischerer Damenkleidung, die der aktiveren Rolle der Frau in der Gesellschaft Rechnung trug.

Da sich ein Teil der Kundschaft außerdem in schicke Resorts am Meer zurückgezogen hatte, um den Kriegsunruhen zu entgehen, eröffnete Jeanne Lanvin Anfang 1916 ihre ersten Geschäfte in den Küstenorten Deauville und Biarritz.

Das Jahr 1917 war weltweit von großen Umbrüchen geprägt. Einerseits waren die USA auf Seiten der Alliierten dem Krieg beigetreten. Andererseits zog sich das im revolutionären Chaos steckende Russland aus dem Konflikt zurück. Nur wenige waren sich zu diesem Zeitpunkt bewusst, dass eben jene Revolution, die später zum Bürgerkrieg führen sollte, den Verlust einer bedeutenden Kundengruppe bedeuten würde. Der russische Adel und das wohlhabende Industriellenbürgertum waren stets Anhänger der französischen Mode gewesen. Für Jeanne Lanvin und ihre Tochter ging 1917 jedoch ein Traum in Erfüllung. Am 21. Mai heiratete Marguerite ihre große Liebe aus Kindheitstagen, René Jacquemaire-Clémenceau. Sie hatte drei Jahre auf diesen Moment warten müssen, nachdem der Medizinstudent René 1914 an die Front gerufen worden war. Dass der Großvater des Bräutigams, Georges Clémenceau, der beliebteste französische Politiker seiner Zeit, der kurz vor seiner zweiten Amtszeit als Ministerpräsident stand, bei der Feier anwesend war, zeugte von dem eindrucksvollen gesellschaftlichen Aufstieg, den Jeanne Lanvin in den letzten 30 Jahren zurückgelegt hatte. Doch ihre erfolgreichsten Jahre lagen noch vor ihr.

Lanvin blue: colours in Jeanne Lanvin's vision of fashion

Jeanne Lanvin not only drew her inspiration from historical costumes, but also paid particular attention to paintings for her choices of colours. Two periods, in particular, seemed to inspire her: that of the Renaissance masters and the more modern period of the impressionists and symbolists, to which the contemplation of the stained-glass windows in the gothic cathedrals could be added. Her regular stays in Italy had allowed her to discover for herself the beauty of the colours used by the Italian masters and work out how to reproduce them successfully on fabrics. To reach this goal, she decided to open a dye factory in Nanterre, near Paris, in 1923. Subsequently, the factory was also used for the development of perfumes by the Lanvin brand. The extensive library in her office contained several books offering detailed colour charts, allowing her to familiarise herself with very subtle shades.

While she was interested in the full range of colours, Jeanne Lanvin seemed to have developed a particular fascination for blue. Almost thirty different shades of blue were recorded in the dresses and other garments she designed. Above all, after the beginning of the First World War, a blue-grey shade, known as horizon blue, which was worn by French soldiers, became the patriotic colour par excellence, and women's fashion took it up. The signature shade of blue now associated with the brand, the famous Lanvin blue, was a medium dark blue with glints of mauve. That colour seems to have been inspired by the work of Fra Angelico (1395-1455), where it was frequently used in the depiction of clothes, but also by the blue of medieval stained-glass windows, with the play of sunrays that lightened or darkened the panes in an infinite series

of hues. As with all of Jeanne Lanvin's work, this was not a direct and simple take on the colour invented by Fra Angelico, but rather a reinterpretation of a blue that she had also seen in liturgical vestments, another of her regular sources for shapes and embroidery. For the bedroom and boudoir of her Parisian mansion at rue Barbet-de-Jouy, Jeanne Lanvin chose, in the mid-1920s, a dark ultramarine blue, more intense than the Lanvin blue, which she decided to complement with ivory hues.

p. 100: Fra Angelico, *Coronation of the Virgin*, 1434-1435. Musée du Louvre, Paris.

S. 100: Fra Angelico, *Die Krönung der Jungfrau*, 1434–1435. Musée du Louvre, Paris.

Dinner dress, 1939.

Formelles Kleid, 1939.

Day dress, slate blue silk crepe, 1909.

Gesellschaftskleid, schieferblauer Seidenkrepp, 1909.

p. 103: *Butterfly* dress, 1924 (sketch).

S. 103: Kleid „Butterfly", 1924 (Skizze).

Lanvin-Blau: Farben in Jeanne Lanvins Vision der Mode

Jeanne Lanvin ließ sich nicht nur von historischen Trachten inspirieren, sondern orientierte sich bei der Farbwahl auch gern an Gemälden. Insbesondere die großen Meister der Renaissance und die etwas moderneren Impressionisten und Symbolisten schienen sie zu inspirieren, und auch die Buntglasfenster gotischer Kirchen gefielen ihr. Bei ihren regelmäßigen Aufenthalten in Italien hatte sie die Schönheit der Farben entdeckt, die von den großen Meistern häufig

verwendet wurden, und gelernt, diese Farben für ihre Stoffe zu verwenden. Dafür eröffnete sie 1923 in Nanterre in der Nähe von Paris eine Fabrik zur Farbherstellung. Später wurden in dieser Fabrik auch ihre Parfums hergestellt. In der großen Bibliothek in Jeannes Büro gab es gleich mehrere Bücher mit detaillierten Farbkarten, so dass sie die gesamte Farbpalette mit all ihren subtilen Schattierungen stets zur Hand hatte.

Obwohl Jeanne Lanvin sich grundsätzlich für das gesamte Farbspektrum interessierte, war sie von der Farbe Blau doch besonders fasziniert. Fast 30 verschiedene Blautöne wurden in ihren Entwürfen festgestellt. Kurz nach Beginn des ersten Weltkriegs wurde eine grau-blaue Nuance, die auch unter dem Namen Horizontblau bekannt ist, *die* Farbe des Patriotismus, da sie von den französischen Soldaten getragen wurde. Auch in die Damenmode hielt dieser Farbton Einzug. Das charakteristische Lanvin-Blau, das bis heute mit der Marke in Verbindung gebracht wird, war ein mitteldunkles, fliederfarbenes Blau. Die Inspiration für den Farbton kam vermutlich vom italienischen Maler Fra Angelico (1395-1455), der ihn oft für die Darstellung von Kleidern einsetzte. Auch das Blau mittelalterlicher Glasmalerei, das je nach Lichteinfall heller oder dunkler wirkte und eine schier unendliche Zahl an Schattierungen hervorbrachte, spielte möglicherweise eine Rolle. Wie auch sonst in Jeanne Lanvins Schaffen wurde die Farbe von Fra Angelico aber nicht einfach übernommen, sondern neu interpretiert. Auch in liturgischen Gewändern, die regelmäßig Inspiration für Schnittformen und Stickereien lieferten, kam der Farbton gelegentlich vor. Das Schlafzimmer und Ankleidezimmer ihres Pariser Wohnsitzes in der Rue Barbet-de-Jouy ließ Jeanne Lanvin in ein dunkles Marineblau tünchen, das noch intensiver als das Lanvin-Blau war, und setzte dazu elfenbeinfarbige Akzente.

"She has taken from
the humble Fra Angelico
a little of his heavenly blue."

La Gazette du Bon Ton, 1925,
about Jeanne Lanvin's signature blue

„Sie nahm dem demütigen
Fra Angelico ein bisschen
seines himmlischen
Blautons."

La Gazette du Bon Ton, 1925,
über Jeanne Lanvins charakteristisches Blau

p. 106: Afternoon dress, 1924.

S. 106: Gesellschaftskleid, 1924.

Jeanne Lanvin's Polignac pink was inspired, among other sources, by Pierre Bonnard's paintings such as *Jardin au Cannet*.

Für den Farbton Polignac-Rosa ließ sich Jeanne Lanvins u. a. von Pierre Bonnards Gemälden wie *Jardin au Cannet* inspirieren.

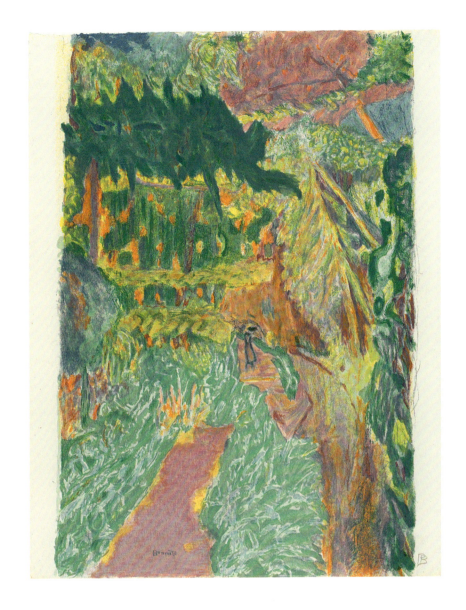

Another colour associated with Jeanne Lanvin is Polignac pink, a bright, pale coral rose she created in honour of her daughter. Its name is associated with the aristocratic family of Count Jean de Polignac, Marguerite's second husband, whom she married in 1924. Here, the hue seemed to have been inspired by the slightly pearly pink in Pierre Bonnard's paintings. In the same way, Jeanne Lanvin made a point of recreating the characteristic green used by Diego Vélazquez, and was marked, in her choices of red, by the palettes of Renoir and Cézanne. It is also known that she was influenced by the delicate shades of colours found in the paintings by Odilon Redon, a symbolist painter she highly valued.

Eine weitere Farbe, die oft mit Jeanne Lanvin in Verbindung gebracht wird, ist Polignac, ein helles, blasses Altrosa, das sie zu Ehren ihrer Tochter kreiert hatte. Benannt wurde es nach dem Grafen Jean de Polignac, Marguerites zweitem Ehemann, den sie 1924 heiratete. In diesem Fall erinnert die Nuance an das Korallenrosa, das in den Gemälden des zeitgenössischen Malers Pierre Bonnard gerne zum Einsatz kam. Jeanne Lanvin verwendete in ihren Kreationen außerdem das charakteristische Grün aus den Werken des spanischen Malers Diego Velázquez und ließ sich in der Wahl ihrer Rottöne von den Farbpaletten Renoirs und Cézannes inspirieren. Auch Odilon Redon, ein von ihr sehr geschätzter Künstler des Symbolismus, beeinflusste sie mit den zarten Nuancen seiner Gemälde.

1920-1929

The Triumphant Decade

Das Jahrzehnt des Triumphs

"Paris, Lanvin! Two names I love because they evoke so many beautiful things for me. What I found here? Very youthful dresses as I like them and a harmonious understanding of colours."

American Actress Mary Pickford
in an interview with French *Vogue*, September 1924

„Paris, Lanvin! Diese beiden Namen liebe ich, weil sie so viel Schönes heraufbeschwören. Was ich dort fand? Jugendliche Kleider, wie ich sie am liebsten mag, und ein Verständnis für das harmonische Zusammenspiel der Faben."

Die amerikanische Schauspielerin Mary Pickford
in einem Interview mit der Französischen
Vogue, September 1924

"Jeanne Lanvin – Faubourg St. Honoré
Madame Jeanne Lavin was formerly a
successful milliner, but for the past few
years has come to the front as a producer
of successful models that are of the type
referred to as 'Little dresses' frocks of
simple and girlish and becoming lines.
The Lanvin dress is always marked
by some original touch."

Dressmakers Dictionary, 1916
Published by J. W. Goddard & Sons, New York

This glowing description of Jeanne Lanvin's
activities, meant for the New York fashion
scene, perfectly summarised, with an
American touch of concision, the amazing
career the couturier had achieved since
opening her first millinery shop in 1889.
Some of her colleagues, however, were
granted slightly more critical observations,
such as Paul Poiret, who was "noted for his
extreme and sometimes eccentric dress
conceptions; daring in colour scheme
as well as design." A few years later, the
Gazette du Bon Ton celebrated the elegance
of the Lanvin collections with similar
accolades: "Madame Lanvin showed us
in one hour, and without any wrong note,
frocks in the fashion of 1925, robes de style
and gowns for children and girls. And her
approach was so personal – a combination
of taste, moderation, and refinement –
that we were never, even for a moment,
disconcerted by this amazing feat, which
on the contrary has remained an instant
of pure grace and harmony".

„Jeanne Lanvin – Faubourg Saint-Honoré
Madame Lanvin war ehemals erfolgreiche
Hutmacherin, etablierte sich in den letzten
Jahren aber mit der Anfertigung
erfolgreicher Modelle, die als „kleine
Kleider" bekannt sind: schlichte,
mädchenhafte Kleider mit schmeichelnder
Linienführung. Kleider von Lanvin zeichnen
sich stets durch ein originelles Detail aus."

Schneidereihandbuch
Dressmakers Dictionary, 1916
Verlag: J. W. Goddard & Sons, New York

Diese wohlwollende, für die New Yorker
Modeszene bestimmte Beschreibung
fasst kurz und knapp zusammen, was
Jeanne Lanvin seit Eröffnung ihres ersten
Hutmachergeschäfts 1889 erreicht hat.
Einige ihrer Kollegen, darunter Paul Poiret,
wurden hingegen auf etwas kritischere
Weise beschrieben. So hieß es über
Poiret, er sei „für extreme und zuweilen
exzentrische Entwürfe bekannt und bei
Farben sowie Design sehr wagemutig".
Jahre später wurde Jeanne Lanvin in
der *Gazette du Bon Ton* erneut in höchsten
Tönen gepriesen: „In nur einer Stunde
zeigte uns Madame Lanvin ohne falsche
Umschweife, was man 1925 trägt, ihre
Robes de style und Abendkleider für Frauen
und Mädchen. Angesichts ihres durchaus
persönlichen Ansatzes – eine Kombination
aus gutem Geschmack, Maß und Raffinesse
– ist ihr bemerkenswerter Erfolg nur allzu
gut nachvollziehbar. Für uns ein Erlebnis
voller Anmut und Harmonie."

Art - Goût - Beauté

THE TRIUMPHANT DECADE / DAS JAHRZEHNT DES TRIUMPHS (1920–1929)

p. 114: *A dinner at the Ritz*, fashion illustration with dresses by Jeanne Lanvin, 1924.

S. 114: *Ein Abendessen im Ritz*, Modeillustration mit Kleidern von Jeanne Lanvin, 1924.

p. 115: *Robe de style*, early 1920s.

S. 115: *Robe de style*. Frühe 1920er Jahre.

Fashion inspired
by *La Garçonne,*
around 1923.

Von *La Garçonne*
inspirierte Kleidung,
ca. 1923.

In November 1919, the world had emerged from a long war whose atrocities and countless casualties had deeply affected people's minds. The conflict led to the fall of the German Empire and Austria-Hungary, plunged Russia into revolutionary turmoil, and consecrated the new leading role of the United States in world affairs initiated under the presidency of Woodrow Wilson (1856-1924). In France, as in other countries, the euphoria caused by the victory could not erase all the suffering of the soldiers who had returned from the front disillusioned and traumatised by what they had experienced for four years. Injured and crippled veterans haunted the streets of towns and villages, bearing witness to the absurdity of the war, and struggling to reintegrate into a society for which they had sacrificed themselves. The war had also changed the role and image of women, who had been called upon to replace, in all spheres of activity, the men who had left for the front. The emancipation of women, which had begun before the war with the suffragettes, had suddenly accelerated, and this momentum was reflected in the trend for shorter hairstyles that tallied with the demand for equality between men and women. In the autumn of 1922, a novel by a feminist writer and left-wing sympathiser, Victor Margueritte, *La Garçonne*, was published, describing the emancipation of a young girl who has broken off an arranged engagement to live as she chooses. The free lifestyle she adopted in the course of the chapters –

having affairs with both female and male partners, running her own successful business, driving a car and smoking opium – caused such a scandal that the author, who had been awarded the Légion d'Honneur during the war for his bravery, was struck off the order, an extremely rare decision usually reserved for those sentenced to prison. The impact of the scandal, however, contributed to the book's instant success throughout the western world, and the story's protagonist, Monique Lerbier, became a role model for a generation of young women who wanted to break free from the shackles of social convention.

Was it a coincidence that, in the same year, Marguerite divorced her first husband René Jacquemaire? Interestingly, she adopted some of the attitudes of the *garçonne* – she was known for her addiction to opium – and devoted herself to her passion for music. An independent woman who had divorced her first husband and lived separated from her second, Jeanne Lanvin, while not taking sides publicly, seemed to support the *garçonnes* by designing outfits in the provocative spirit of their trend, although without going so far as to design women's trousers. And she never neglected the more classic shapes, especially the romantic *robe de style* with its narrow waist and full skirt that evoked the pannier dresses of the 18th century, nor the straight, slender, modern dresses that were all the rage at the time. It seemed that, for Jeanne Lanvin, the choice of a dress shape was

more a question of trend and the client's personal taste: what mattered was the quality of the fabric, the perfection of the cut, the refinement of the decoration, and exquisite originality. Fashion was also meant to mirror the spirit of the times, as she said in an interview at the end of 1925: "A great dressmaker does not work heedlessly. He does not believe in art for art's sake. The dress must be suitable to the contemporary woman, to that of 1925 and not another. To a society of sport, of accelerated haste, of perpetual movement we shall not recommend the crinoline or long trains." However, "what the woman of taste requires is a dress which appears new without being so, something undefinable and which is, every time, as Verlaine says, neither quite the same, nor quite another." Always on the move, always on the alert, Jeanne Lanvin's spirit was well attuned to the frantic rhythm of the Roaring Twenties, rocked by hot jazz and the Charleston. The success she had built up slowly and cautiously over the previous decade suddenly went through the roof in a dizzying upward spiral. The early 1920s marked the apotheosis of her professional career. The decade between the armistice and the financial crisis of 1929 saw the golden age of the Lanvin brand, a success driven by *joie de vivre* and insouciance, which had gradually regained their rightful place in society after years of pain and grief.

Im November 1919 war die Welt gezeichnet
von einem Krieg, dessen Gräuel und
zahllose Todesopfer die Menschen
zutiefst erschütterten. Der Krieg hatte
zum Zusammenbruch des Deutschen
Kaiserreichs sowie Österreich-Ungarns
geführt, Russland in revolutionäre
Unruhen gestürzt und den internationalen
Führungsanspruch der USA unter Woodrow
Wilson (1856-1924) untermauert.
In Frankreich, wie in anderen Ländern
auch, konnte die Siegeseuphorie das
Leid der Soldaten, die desillusioniert und
traumatisiert von der Front zurückkehrten,
nicht ungeschehen machen. Die Straßen
in den Städten und Dörfern waren voller
verletzter und verstümmelter Veteranen,
die von der Absurdität des Krieges
zeugten und sich nur schwer wieder in
die Gesellschaft, für die sie sich geopfert
hatten, eingliedern konnten. Ganz nebenbei
hatte der Krieg große Auswirkungen auf die
Rolle der Frauen, die in den verschiedensten
Berufen die an die Front gezogenen Männer
ersetzen mussten. Die Emanzipation der
Frau, die durch die Suffragetten bereits vor
dem Krieg begonnen hatte, wurde dadurch
beschleunigt. Diese Entwicklung spiegelte
sich auch in den Kurzhaarschnitten
der Frauen wider, die damit die Forderung
nach mehr Gleichberechtigung untermalten.
Im Herbst 1922 veröffentlichte der
linke feministische Schriftsteller Victor
Margueritte seinen Roman *La Garçonne*,
in dem es um die Emanzipation einer
jungen Frau geht, die ihre Verlobung auflöst,
um stattdessen über ihr eigenes Leben
zu bestimmen. Das Buch beschreibt das
freie Leben der Protagonistin: Sie beginnt
Liebesbeziehungen sowohl mit Männern
als auch mit Frauen, führt ein eigenes

A Garçonne-style suit,
mid-1920s.

Kostüm im Garçonne-Stil,
Mitte der 1920er Jahre.

Unternehmen, fährt Auto und raucht Opium. Diese Beschreibungen lösten einen derartigen Skandal aus, dass dem Autor, der für seinen Kriegsdienst mit dem Orden der *Légion d'Honneur* ausgezeichnet worden war, dieser Titel wieder entzogen wurde. Eine äußerst seltene Maßnahme, die sonst nur im Fall von Gefängnisstrafen ergriffen wurde. Der Skandal verhalf dem Roman jedoch in der gesamten westlichen Welt zu sofortigem Erfolg und die Hauptfigur Monique Lerbier wurde zum Vorbild einer ganzen Generation junger Frauen, die sich von den Ketten der gesellschaftlichen Konvention befreien wollten. War es Zufall, dass sich Marguerite im selben Jahr von ihrem ersten Ehemann René Jacquemaire scheiden ließ? Tatsächlich erinnert so mancher Aspekt ihres Lebens an die *Garçonne*. Marguerite war bekanntermaßen opiumsüchtig und beschloss, sich ganz ihrer großen Leidenschaft, der Musik zu verschreiben. Als unabhängige Frau, die von ihrem ersten Mann geschieden war und getrennt von ihrem zweiten Ehemann lebte, äußerte sich Jeanne Lanvin zwar nicht öffentlich zu der Debatte, ihre teilweise doch recht provokanten Kreationen können jedoch als Unterstützung für die *Garçonnes* gelesen werden. So weit, Damenhosen zu entwerfen, ging sie jedoch nicht. Auch die klassischen Schnitte ließ sie nicht außer Acht, weder die *Robe de style* mit der schmalen Taille und dem vollen Rock, der an die Reifröcke des 18. Jahrhunderts erinnerte, noch die modernen, schmal geschnittenen Kleider, die gerade sehr in Mode waren.

Die Wahl der Kleiderform war für Jeanne Lanvin offenbar in erster Linie eine Frage des aktuellen Trends sowie der Vorlieben der jeweiligen Kundinnen. Weitaus wichtiger waren ihr die Stoffqualität, der perfekte Schnitt, die feinen Verzierungen und die Einzigartigkeit der Stücke. Wie sie in einem Interview Ende 1925 sagte, betrachtete sie Mode als einen Spiegel der Zeit: „Eine erfolgreiche Modeschöpferin muss sehr besonnen arbeiten. Sie glaubt nicht an die Kunst um der Kunst willen. Das Kleid muss zu den Frauen unserer Zeit passen – zu den Frauen des Jahres 1925, zu keinen anderen. In einer aktiven, schnelllebigen Gesellschaft, die ständig in Bewegung ist, dürfen wir nicht zu Reifröcken oder langen Schleppen raten." Sie sagte jedoch auch: „Eine Frau mit gutem Geschmack braucht ein Kleid, das neu wirkt, ohne es zu sein. Es hat etwas Undefinierbares, das, wie Verlaine es formuliert, weder ganz gleich noch völlig neu ist." Ständig in Bewegung und am Puls der Zeit, passte Jeanne Lanvin gut in die Goldenen Zwanziger mit ihrem schnellen Rhythmus, heißem Jazz und Charleston. Ihr mühsam und beständig aufgebauter Erfolg der letzten Jahre nahm plötzlich eine ganz neue Dynamik an. In den frühen Zwanzigern stand sie am Gipfel ihrer Karriere. Die zehn Jahre zwischen dem Ende des Ersten Weltkriegs und dem Beginn der Weltwirtschaftskrise 1929 waren das goldene Zeitalter der Marke Lanvin. Den großen Erfolg verdankte Lanvin der Sorglosigkeit und Lebensfreude, die nach Jahren der Trauer und des Schmerzes wieder ihren Platz in der Gesellschaft gefunden hatten.

Roseraie silk dress, 1923.
Details of the ornamental
patterns.

Seidenkleid „Roseraie",
1923. Detailansichten
der Verzierungen.

By 1921, the Lanvin company already occupied the entire building at 22 rue du Faubourg Saint-Honoré, but the premises had become inadequate for the hundreds of employees who worked there every day. The issue was creatively solved by Jeanne Lanvin: She had the building raised by one more floor, and acquired part of a nearby house at 15 rue Saint Honoré – an address she knew well, for she had spent several years there as an apprentice in Madame Felix's milliner's workshop. Her plan was to open a new boutique, dedicated to interior decoration, in partnership with young designer and decorator Armand-Albert Rateau, who would subsequently refurbish all her boutiques and design Jeanne Lanvin's interiors in her Parisian mansion. Although Rateau's clientele already included the European and North American élite, and the two partners were both pragmatic, astute businesspeople, the company was not to succeed in operating profitably and closed four years later, but this semi-failure affected neither the good relationship between Jeanne Lanvin and the talented decorator nor their lasting friendship. Jeanne Lanvin was thus able to assess the influence of Art Deco in the aesthetic and drew inspiration from its principles to invent original decorative motifs. Geometric shapes typical of the Bauhaus style were present in certain models. More generally, the lines and shapes became more restrained and sleeker, like the simple and elegant cloche hat, adopted by women with short hair, for whom it was perfectly suited, and which Jeanne Lanvin fashioned in multiple versions over the following decades.

Im Jahr 1921 hatte die Firma Lanvin bereits das gesamte Gebäude der Nummer 22 in der Rue du Faubourg Saint-Honoré übernommen. Dennoch reichte der Platz nicht mehr für die hunderten Angestellten, die hier ihrer täglichen Arbeit nachgingen. Jeanne Lanvin löste das Problem auf kreative Weise: Sie ließ ein zusätzliches Stockwerk auf das Gebäude bauen und kaufte außerdem einen Teil des nahegelegenen Hauses in Nummer 15. Diese Adresse kannte sie bereits gut, da sie hier mehrere Jahre als Lehrling in der Hutmacherwerkstatt von Madame Félix gearbeitet hatte. Ihr Plan war es, hier eine Boutique nur für Inneneinrichtung zu eröffnen. Dazu ging sie eine Partnerschaft mit dem jungen Innenarchitekten und Dekorateur Armand-Albert Rateau ein, der später die Renovation all ihrer Geschäfte und die Gestaltung ihrer Pariser Wohnung übernehmen sollte. Obwohl Rateau die Elite Nordamerikas und Europas zu seiner Kundschaft zählte und beide Kooperationspartner pragmatische und fähige Geschäftsleute waren, scheiterte das Unterfangen. Da es nicht profitabel war, wurde das Geschäft nach vier Jahren wieder geschlossen. Dieser Misserfolg sollte dem guten Verhältnis und der Freundschaft zwischen den beiden jedoch nicht schaden. Durch ihren Kontakt zu dem talentierten Dekorateur war Jeanne Lanvin in der Lage, den Einfluss des Art déco auf die zeitgenössische Ästhetik besser einschätzen zu können, und ließ sich davon inspirieren, originelle neue Motive zu entwickeln. In einigen Modellen spiegelten sich die für den Bauhausstil typischen geometrischen Formen wider. Grundsätzlich wurden die Formen und Linien glatter und schnittiger. Der simple, elegante Topfhut, der so gut zu Frauen mit kurzen Haaren passte, ist dafür das perfekte Beispiel. Jeanne Lanvin brachte im Laufe der Jahrzehnte verschiedene Versionen dieses Hutes heraus.

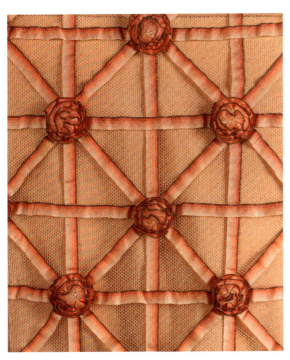

Embroidered handbag,
1925.

Reich verzierte
Handtasche, 1925.

pp. 124-125: Evening
ensemble, 1923.

S. 124-125:
Abendgarderobe, 1923.

pp. 126-127: Summer
evening dresses, 1923.

S. 126-127: Abendkleider
für den Sommer, 1923.

Evening dress, 1924.

Abendkleid, 1924.

Always striving to push the boundaries of perfection, she opened a dye factory in Nanterre, near Paris, in 1923, which allowed her to master the art of colouring textiles and to play with the subtle differences in hues. She later set up her perfume laboratory at the same place, under the direction of André Fraysse, the legendary perfume-creating "nose" of the brand, working with him to develop all of the company's celebrated fragrances. A far-sighted woman, Jeanne Lanvin commissioned the illustrator Paul Iribe, one of the regular contributors to the *Gazette du Bon Ton* – who also went down in history as one of Coco Chanel's most enduring lovers – to create a logo for the future perfumes. Iribe's choice – or perhaps Jeanne Lanvin's – was to depict a woman and a little girl, both dressed for a masquerade ball, facing each other and holding hands. It looked as if Iribe had borrowed the subject from a 1907 photograph of the 10-year-old Marguerite and her mother, both dressed in billowing black dresses and wearing fairy hats. The origin of the photograph, however, is not attested. This logo would henceforth be featured on the company's letterhead and adorned all perfume bottles, starting with *My Sin*, launched in 1924 for the American market. The history of this feminine, provocative, and dangerously seductive fragrance has been shrouded in mystery. Its creator was said to have been a Russian emigrant, Madame Zed, a perfumer who obviously liked to be secretive, for nothing is known of her except for this strange nickname. However, it turned out to be a resounding commercial success, and Jeanne Lanvin asked the newly appointed André Fraysse to create a perfume in honour of her daughter's thirtieth birthday in 1927. The soft and balanced fragrance, called *Arpège*, with notes of Bulgarian rose, Grasse jasmine, honeysuckle and lily of the valley, was indeed an olfactory arpeggio where the scents united in a perfect accord. Marguerite, Jeanne's beloved daughter, married Count Jean de Polignac in 1924, a music-loving aristocrat with a passion for literature whose family history dated back to the Middle Ages and whose fortune owed much to his mother, the sole heiress

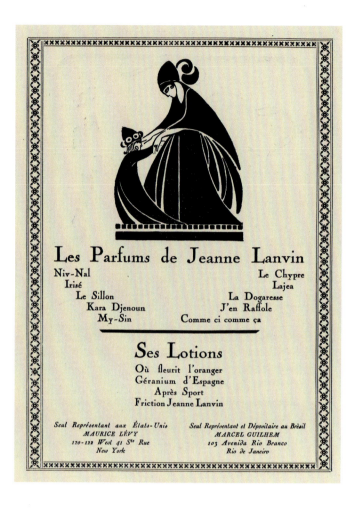

of Pommery champagnes. To mark her entry into the most exclusive aristocratic circles, Marguerite, at her husband's suggestion, changed her first name and would be called by her other two names, Marie-Blanche. While Marguerite's first marriage had established the Lanvin family's entry into the circles of power, the second had opened the doors of the most select Parisian salons to Jeanne, and the entire Polignac family was henceforth dressed in Lanvin, since a new department for men's fashion had opened in 1925 at the former address of Lanvin Décoration. Despite the whirlwind of cultural and social life she was caught up in, Jeanne Lanvin did not neglect her highly successful business and continued to innovate and expand: in 1924 she opened boutiques in Cannes and Le Touquet, then launched, in addition to the men's department, a sportswear boutique in 1925.

p. 130: Advertising for Lanvin's perfumes,
late 1920s.

S. 130: Werbung für Lanvins Parfums,
späte 1920er Jahre.

Left: French actress Maud Loti in a dress
designed by Jeanne Lanvin, 1922.

Links: Die französische Schauspielerin Maud
Loti in einem von Jeanne Lanvin entworfenen
Kleid, 1922.

Right: Theatrical dress for French actress Jane
Renouardt, 1927.

Rechts: Theaterkleider für die französische
Schauspielerin Jane Renouardt, 1927.

p. 132: *Vogue* swimsuit, 1924. One of the first examples of sportswear in Jeanne Lanvin's oeuvre.

S. 132: Badeanzug „Vogue", 1924. Eines der ersten Beispiele für Sportkleidung in Jeanne Lanvins Schaffen.

Neptune dress, designed for the boutiques at the sea resorts, 1926.

Kleid „Neptune", für Boutiquen in den Resorts am Meer entworfen, 1926.

Février 1924

Février 1924

MONT ROSE

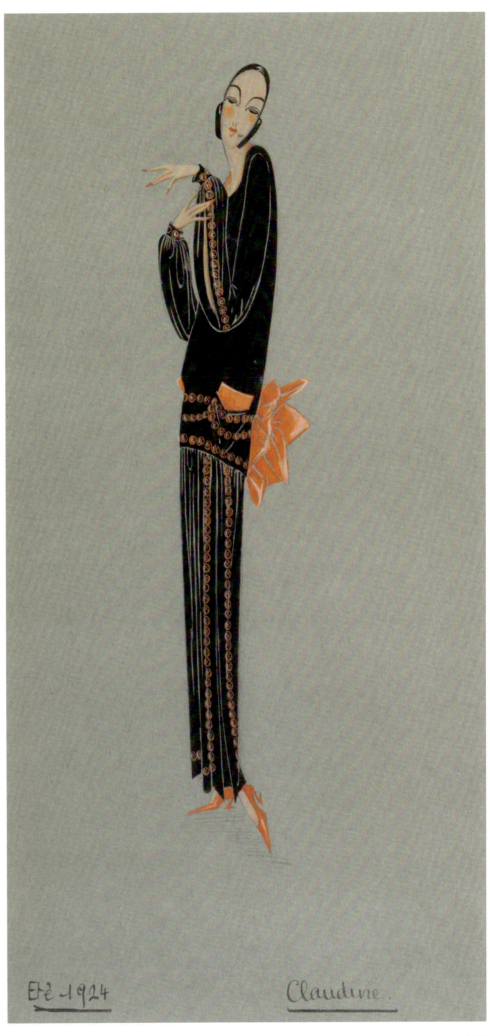

p. 134: Evening dresses
(sketches), 1924.

S. 134: Abendkleider
(Skizzen), 1924.

Claudine summer dress
(sketch), 1924.

Sommerkleid „Claudine"
(Skizze), 1924.

p. 136:
Day ensemble, 1920s.

S. 136: Tagesoutfit,
1920er Jahre.

Summer coat, 1924.

Mantel für den Sommer,
1924.

SPORT 8. —
Crêpe du Maroc.
Jean Patou.

CIMA ROSA. —
Crêpe imprimé.
Jeanne Lanvin.

Top: *Cima Rosa* dress (sketch), 1929.

Oben: Kleid „Cima Rosa" (Skizze), 1929.

Bottom: *Donatienne* dress (sketch), 1929.

Unten: Kleid „Donatienne" (Skizze), 1929.

p. 139: *Saphir* dress (sketch), 1929.

S. 139: Kleid „Saphir" (Skizze), 1929.

BOUQUETS DE FLEURS. —
Mousseline imprimée.
Jean Patou.

DONATIENNE. —
Velours imprimé.
Jeanne Lanvin.

SAPHIR. —
Tulle et paillette acier.
Jeanne Lanvin.

Auf der ständigen Suche nach Perfektion
eröffnete sie 1923 eine Farbfabrik
in Nanterre in der Nähe von Paris.
Jetzt war sie in der Lage, die Kunst
der Textilfärbung zu erlernen und mit den
subtilen Unterschieden zwischen einzelnen
Schattierungen zu spielen. Später wurde an
dem Standort außerdem das Parfumlabor
unter der Leitung von André Fraysse
eingerichtet. Fraysse war die legendäre
„Nase" der Marke und an der Entwicklung
der berühmtesten Düfte beteiligt.
Vorausschauend wie sie war, beauftragte
Jeanne Lanvin den Illustrator Paul Iribe, ein
Logo für die Parfums zu entwerfen.
Iribe arbeitete regelmäßig für die *Gazette
du Bon Ton* und ging als einer der Liebhaber
Coco Chanels in die Geschichte ein. Seine
Wahl – oder womöglich Jeanne Lanvins
Wahl – fiel auf die stilisierte Darstellung
einer Frau und eines kleinen Mädchens,
die beide festlich gekleidet sind und sich an
den Händen halten. Vermutlich hat Iribe das
Motiv von einem 1907 entstandenen Foto
adaptiert, das die 10-jährige Marguerite
und ihre Mutter in weiten schwarzen

Kleidern und Feenhüten zeigt. Woher dieses
Foto stammt, ist nicht bekannt. Das Logo
fand sich von nun an auf dem Briefkopf der
Firma und zierte alle Parfumflakons. Das
erste Parfum, *My Sin*, kam 1924 in Amerika
auf den Markt. Wie dieser weibliche,
provokante, gefährlich verführerische Duft
entstanden ist, ist bis heute ein Rätsel.
Es heißt, dass eine russische Emigrantin
namens Madame Zed den Duft kreiert
haben soll. Sie muss eine Parfümeurin
gewesen sein, die das Rampenlicht mied,
da außer diesem Namen nichts über sie
bekannt ist. Das Parfum erwies sich als
ein großer Verkaufserfolg und Jeanne
bat den gerade neu eingestellten André
Fraysse, zu Ehren von Marguerites 30.
Geburtstag im Jahr 1927 einen eigenen
Duft zu kreieren. Der sanfte, wunderbar
ausgewogene Duft namens *Arpège*, mit
Noten bulgarischer Rose, Grasse-Jasmin,
Geißblatt und Maiglöckchen, war – wie
der Name schon sagte – in der Tat ein
Arpeggio für den Geruchssinn. Jeannes
geliebte Tochter Marguerite heiratete
1924 den Grafen Jean de Polignac, einen
Adligen mit einer Leidenschaft für Musik
und Literatur, dessen Stammbaum sich
bis ins Mittelalter zurückverfolgen ließ.
Sein Vermögen verdankte er seiner Mutter,
der Alleinerbin der Champagnermarke
Pommery. Anlässlich der Aufnahme
in die exklusivsten Adelskreise schlug
Marguerites neuer Ehemann ihr vor, ihren
Namen zu ändern. Von da an wurde sie bei
ihrem zweiten Vornamen Marie-Blanche
gerufen. Nachdem Marguerites erste Ehe
der Familie Lanvin Zugang zu den Kreisen
der Mächtigen verschafft hatte, öffnete die
zweite Ehe die Türen zu erlesenen Pariser
Salons. Bald war die ganze Familie Polignac
in Lanvin gekleidet, nachdem 1925 die neue
Abteilung für Herrenmode am ehemaligen
Standort von *Lanvin Décoration* eröffnet
wurde. Trotz der vielen gesellschaftlichen
und kulturellen Umbrüche, die sich zu ihrer
Lebenszeit ereigneten, behielt Jeanne
Lanvin die Entwicklung ihres Unternehmen
stets im Blick. Sie blieb innovativ und
expandierte mehrmals. 1924 eröffnete
sie je ein Geschäft in Cannes und
Le Touquet. 1925 eröffnete sie neben
der neuen Herrenabteilung außerdem
ein Geschäft für Sportkleidung.

Hollywood star Gilda Gray in an evening dress
by Jeanne Lanvin, around 1924.

Hollywood-Star Gilda Gray in einem von
Jeanne Lanvin entworfenen Abendkleid, ca. 1924.

p. 141: Music Hall dancer Mademoiselle Rahna
in a Lanvin dress, 1924.

S. 141: Variété-Tänzerin Mademoiselle Rahna
in einem Kleid von Lanvin, 1924.

Evening dress, 1928.

Abendkleid, 1928.

p. 143:
Evening dress, 1929.

p. 143: Abendkleid, 1929.

In 1925, as Jeanne Lanvin was the head of the haute couture section at the Exposition Internationale des Arts Décoratifs Modernes in Paris, her brand employed more than 800 people and had no less than 23 different workshops. These remarkable achievements earned Jeanne Lanvin the Légion d'Honneur the following year, a well-deserved distinction on the threshold of her sixties (she was promoted to Officer of the same order in 1938 as an ultimate recognition of her merits).

In the late 1920s, perhaps on the occasion of her sixtieth birthday, Jeanne Lanvin set off on a holiday trip to Egypt. A photograph taken in Giza showed her sitting on the hump of a dromedary, her back to the pyramids, and her gaze lost in the distance, like a sphinx, as if she were about to enter immortality.

Als Jeanne Lanvin 1925 den Bereich der Haute Couture bei der Internationalen Ausstellung für moderne dekorative Kunst und Kunstgewerbe in Paris leitete, zählte ihr Unternehmen mehr als 800 Angestellte sowie 23 Werkstätten. Angesichts ihres großen Erfolgs wurde Jeanne im darauffolgenden Jahr mit dem Verdienstorden der *Légion d'Honneur* ausgezeichnet, eine außerordentliche Ehre, die ihr kurz vor ihrem 60. Geburtstag zuteilwurde. 1938 wurde sie zur Offizierin des Ordens ernannt, um ihren Verdienst mit einer noch höheren Auszeichnung zu würdigen.

In den späten Zwanzigerjahren, womöglich anlässlich ihres 60. Geburtstages, unternahm Jeanne Lanvin eine Reise nach Ägypten. Es gibt ein Foto von dieser Reise, das sie auf einem Dromedar sitzend zeigt, den Blick wie eine Sphinx in die Ferne gerichtet, als wäre sie auf dem Weg in die Unsterblichkeit.

Chauve-souris ("bat"
in French) dress, 1929.

Kleid „Chauve-souris"
(„Fledermaus"), 1929.

Sigur summer dress, 1929.

Sommerkleid „Sigur", 1929.

p. 147: Back of
the *Koh-i-Noor* dress,
1927.

S. 147: Rückenansicht
des Kleides „Koh-i-Noor",
1927.

THE TRIUMPHANT DECADE / DAS JAHRZEHNT DES TRIUMPHS (1920-1929)

The robe de style, Jeanne Lanvin's signature dress

Die Robe de style, Jeanne Lanvins Markenzeichen

The *robe de style*, characterised by its narrow waist and ample skirt, is the dress design most commonly identified with Jeanne Lanvin's oeuvre, so much so that a journalist from *Vogue* magazine noted in October 1924 "the puffy-skirted design has become the 'Lanvin dress'." From 1918 to the 1940s, and particularly in the 1930s, she designed countless variations of this dress, whose origins are rooted in the tradition of the pannier dress, fashionable in the 18th century, and the crinoline dress that was on trend during the Second Empire. True to Jeanne Lanvin's flair for fusing classical sophistication with modern shapes, the *robe de style* differentiates itself from its predecessors by a shorter skirt – just below the knee – and a more vertical, less three-dimensional bodice than in earlier eras.

In 1938, Jeanne Lanvin explained her dedication to *robe de style* to an interviewer for the women's magazine *Minerva* in these words: "How can we neglect the fashions of the past? They represent all the work, art and thought of the centuries before us. However, they should simply serve to enliven our imagination. We need to adapt them to our modern taste and give a constantly new face to things that are eternally beautiful."

Die *Robe de style,* die sich durch ihre schmale Taille und den vollen Rock auszeichnet, ist die Kreation, die besonders häufig mit Jeanne Lanvins Schaffen in Verbindung gebracht wird. Die *Vogue* schrieb im Oktober 1924 sogar, dass sich „das Kleid mit dem bauschigen Rock zum,Lanvin-Kleid' entwickelt" hatte. Von 1918 bis in die 1940er Jahre, insbesondere jedoch in den 1930er Jahren, entwarf sie zahlreiche Varianten dieses Kleides. Dessen Ursprünge lagen in den besonders breiten Pannier-Kleidern, die im 18. Jahrhundert in Mode gewesen waren, sowie in den Reifröcken, die man im Zweiten Kaiserreich getragen hatte. Wie man es von Jeanne Lanvin kennt, kombiniert die *Robe de style* klassische Raffinesse mit modernen Formen, unterscheidet sich aber durch den kürzeren Rock, der knapp unter dem Knie endet, sowie einen steileren, flacheren Rumpf von ihren Vorgängern.

1938 erklärte Jeanne in einem Interview in der Frauenzeitschrift Minerva, warum sie sich der *Robe de style* so intensiv gewidmet hatte: „Wie könnten wir die Mode der Vergangenheit missachten? Sie steht für die Arbeit, Kunst und Ideen der vorangegangenen Jahrhunderte. Dennoch sollten diese uns lediglich dazu dienen, die Fantasie anzuregen. Wir müssen sie unserem modernen Geschmack anpassen und dem, was ewig schön ist, ständig ein neues Gesicht geben."

French actress Jane Renouardt, one of Jeanne Lanvin's close friends, in a *robe de style*, 1925.

Die französische Schauspielerin Jane Renouardt, eine enge Freundin Jeanne Lanvins, in einer *Robe de style*, 1925.

p. 150: *Robe de style*, 1924.

S. 150: *Robe de style*, 1924.

"How can we neglect the fashions of the past? They represent all the work, art and thought of the centuries before us. However, they should simply serve to enliven our imagination."

Jeanne Lanvin

Robe de style (sketch), 1925.

Robe de style (Skizze), 1925.

p. 153: Four fashion illustrations featuring *robes de style* worn in various settings, early 1920s.

S. 153: Vier Modeillustrationen von *Robes de style* zu verschiedenen Anlässen, frühe 1920er Jahre.

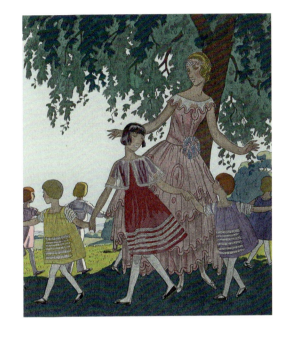

„Wie könnten wir
die Mode der
Vergangenheit missachten?
Sie steht für die Arbeit,
Kunst und Ideen
der vorangegangenen
Jahrhunderte.
Dennoch sollten diese
uns lediglich dazu dienen,
die Fantasie anzuregen.“

Jeanne Lanvin

Original yet without breaking the codes, well adapted to all body shapes and sizes – it conveniently concealed the figure – the robe de style was as appropriate for children as for adults, adding a touch of femininity that Jeanne Lanvin had seemed to miss in the straight and flat dresses of the 1920s. The robe de style thus quickly became a favourite at festive events such as garden parties, weddings, debutante balls, and fancy-dress parties that punctuated the social life of high society. It was, therefore, intended to endow the wearer with a special glow and to stand out for its magnificence.

The shape of the skirt naturally lent itself to the addition of ruffles, providing a sense of light, ethereal movement, while the waist was often adorned with an extravagant ribbon, a flower-shaped cockade, or both. Beaded and embroidered motifs – another characteristic of Jeanne Lanvin's dresses – are used extensively on both the bodice and the skirt. Although it is impossible to list all the embroidered and beaded decorative patterns used by Jeanne Lanvin,

the most frequently utilized ones constitute an eclectic inventory: daisies, roses, tulips, foliage (ivy, olive tree, oak leaves), grapes, stylized crosses – Coptic or Celtic –, arabesques, hearts, seashells, and some geometrical motifs – dots, spirals, lozenges. It is known that Jeanne Lanvin kept several richly illustrated books on botany in her office, from which she drew inspiration. One could certainly trace the influence of the embroidery and decorations seen on liturgical garments, whether of the Roman rite or the Byzantine tradition, as well as of her frequent visits to Gothic cathedrals with their symbolic ornamental friezes.

The whole range of Jeanne Lanvin's favourite colours was used to exalt the delicate beauty of this stylish dress, sometimes with vibrant associations (black and pink, Lanvin blue and gold), even when the dominant colours were blue, coral pink, beige, almond green and mauve. The pale colours were often enhanced with silver threads in the 1920s, in the spirit of Art Déco.

p. 155: *Robe de style* with a large-size cockade, 1927.

S. 155: *Robe de style* mit großer Schleife, 1927.

Robe de style with floral motifs, 1924.

Robe de style mit Blumenmotiven, 1924.

THE ROBE DE STYLE. JEANNE LANVIN'S SIGNATURE DRESS / JEANNE LANVINS MARKENZEICHEN

p. 158: Embroidered *robe de style*, 1922.

S. 158: Verzierte *Robe de style*, 1922.

Jolibois robe de style, 1922.

Robe de style „Jolibois", 1922.

Die *Robe de style* war originell, ohne dabei gegen die Norm zu verstoßen. Sie passte sich allen Körperformen und Größen an und kaschierte bei Bedarf unauffällig. Sie konnte von Kindern ebenso wie von Erwachsenen getragen werden und brachte das feminine Etwas mit, das Jeanne Lanvin in den flachen, geradlinigen Kleidern der zwanziger Jahre vermisste. So wurde sie in der High Society schnell zum Lieblingskleid für Gartenpartys, Hochzeiten, Debütantenbälle und Kostümfeste. Wer die Robe de style trug, wurde von ihr zum Strahlen gebracht und stach aus der Menge heraus.

Der Rock war durch seine Form wie für Volants gemacht, so dass es aussah, als bewege er sich sanft hin und her. Die Taille wurde häufig von einem extravaganten Band, einer blumenförmigen Schleife oder gleich beiden zusammen geziert. Zierperlen und Stickmotive – ein weiteres Markenzeichen der Kleider aus dem Hause Lanvin – wurden sowohl am Rumpf als auch am Rock großzügig eingesetzt. Man kann unmöglich alle Muster aufzählen, die Jeanne Lanvin im Laufe der Zeit kreierte.

Die am häufigsten verwendeten Motive ergeben eine eklektische Sammlung: Margeriten, Rosen, Tulpen, Grünpflanzen (Efeu, Olivenbäume, Eichenblätter), Trauben, stilisierte keltische oder koptische Kreuze, Arabesken, Herzen, Muscheln sowie einige geometrische Muster – Punkte, Spiralen, Rauten. Aus den reich illustrierten Büchern über die Pflanzenwelt, von denen sich gleich mehrere in ihrem Büro befanden, ergab sich für Jeanne Lanvin viel Inspiration. Auch liturgische Gewänder der römischen oder byzantinischen Tradition sowie gotische Kathedralen mit ihren symbolisch verzierten Friesen beeinflussten die Gestaltung ihrer Stickereien und Verzierungen.

Um die zarte Schönheit des Kleides zu unterstreichen, wählte Jeanne Lanvin stets die perfekt passende Farbe aus. Manchmal fiel ihre Wahl auf kräftige Farbtöne (Schwarz und Rosa oder Lanvin-Blau und Gold), doch am häufigsten kamen Blau, Koralle, Beige, Mandelgrün und Malve zum Einsatz. Ganz im Sinne des Art déco wurden die blassen Farben häufig durch silberne Akzentfäden ergänzt.

1930-1939

Constantly Reinventing Fashion

Unermüdliches Neuerfinden

"A superior woman, with an organisational intelligence, gifted with a tact that borders on subtlety; she owes her artistic and moral fortune to her constant will to succeed, without seeking the support of 'patrons' or waiting for a happy chance."

Jeanne Fernandez, in an article on Jeanne Lanvin
for the magazine *L'Art Vivant*, 1931

„Eine herausragende Frau, die mit praktischer Veranlagung, Taktgefühl und Feinheit glänzt. Ihre künstlerische und charakterliche Stärke verdankt sie ihrem eisernen Willen zum Erfolg – ohne je auf die Unterstützung eines Mäzens oder auf das Glück zu warten."

Jeanne Fernandez, in einem Artikel über
Jeanne Lanvin im Magazin *L'Art Vivant*, 1931

The global financial crisis of 1929 marked the abrupt end of the Roaring Twenties and the extravagant, naïvely optimistic atmosphere that had seized the world at the end of the Great War. Just a decade later, and the world was plunged back into uncertainty. International tensions had continued to rise throughout the 1930s, culminating in a new global conflict. French haute couture was hit hard by the Wall Street crash. The wealthy American clientele, who had taken a liking to Parisian fashion, found themselves ruined overnight, and protectionist measures imposed by the American government made imports of luxury goods unaffordable.

The crisis also had a major impact on the French economy, which was slow to recover from the losses of the war and had relied too much on the exorbitant reparations imposed on Germany to keep itself afloat. Paul Poiret, who was already heavily in debt as a result of his lavish lifestyle, and whose collections had been somewhat out of fashion since the mid-1920s, was forced to close his haute couture house in November 1929 and sell off the perfumes that bore his name to pay his debts. As a sign of a bygone era, he published his autobiography *En habillant l'époque* ("Dressing the Time" published in English under the less evocative, but more catchy title "King of Fashion").

Nothing of this nature threatened the brand headed by Jeanne Lanvin. A prudent and smart businesswoman, she had patiently built up her fortune and financial independence, something she had always highly valued, and had sufficiently diversified her activities to avoid exposure to the ups and downs of fashion. As the new decade began, Jeanne Lanvin was already over sixty years old, and had spent no less than fifty years in the fashion industry since her apprenticeship days. Even after so many years, she was still driven to envision all that could still be created and explored rather than looking back nostalgically. As before, she reinvented fashion, designing dresses with a fresh look and with her sharp mind she met the expectations and dreams of her clientele while trying new endeavours, new adventures, such as designing costumes for the cinema. The success of *Arpège* in 1927 encouraged her to launch other perfumes, with the assistance of André Fraysse, who created many of the brand's iconic fragrances over the decade: *Scandal* and *Eau de Lanvin* in 1933, followed by *Rumeur* in 1934 and *Prétexte* in 1937. The perfume business, which had been a creative fantasy in the 1920s, had transformed in the 1930s into a lucrative activity for the Lanvin house. Once again, success crowned Jeanne's efforts.

p. 160: Armenonville suit, 1937.

S. 160: Kostüm „Armenonville", 1937.

p. 162: Jeanne Lanvin at work with a model, 1930s.

S. 162: Jeanne Lanvin bei der Arbeit mit einem Modell, 1930er Jahre.

The entrance to the Lanvin boutique, 1937.

Eingang der Lanvin-Boutique, 1937.

CONSTANTLY REINVENTING FASHION / UNERMÜDLICHES NEUERFINDEN (1930-1939)

Mit dem Beginn der Weltwirtschaftskrise
1929 waren die Goldenen Zwanziger von
einem Moment auf den nächsten vorbei
und mit ihnen auch die naiv hoffnungsvolle,
ausgelassene Stimmung, die die Welt nach
Ende des Ersten Weltkriegs erfasst hatte.
Nur ein Jahrzehnt später wurde die Welt
erneut in große Unsicherheit gestürzt.
Im Laufe der dreißiger Jahre spitzten sich
die internationalen Spannungen immer
weiter zu, bis sie in einen erneuten globalen
Konflikt mündeten. Auch die französische
Haute Couture wurde vom Börsencrash
an der Wall Street in Mitleidenschaft
gezogen. Die wohlhabende amerikanische
Kundschaft, die an der Pariser Mode
Gefallen gefunden hatte, war über Nacht
in den Ruin gestürzt worden. Dazu kam,
dass der Import von Luxusgütern aufgrund
der protektionistischen Maßnahmen
der amerikanischen Regierung
unerschwinglich wurde.

Die Krise wirkte sich zudem massiv auf
die französische Wirtschaft aus. Diese
hatte sich nach den Kriegsverlusten nur
langsam erholt und sich zu sehr auf die
Reparationszahlungen aus Deutschland
verlassen. Paul Poiret, der aufgrund seines
ausschweifenden Lebensstils schon
vorher hoch verschuldet war und dessen
Kollektionen bereits seit Mitte der zwanziger
Jahre nicht mehr in Mode waren, sah sich
im November 1929 gezwungen, sein Haute-
Couture-Haus aufzugeben und die Parfums,
die seinen Namen trugen, zu verkaufen.
Nur so konnte er seine Schulden begleichen.
Im Zeichen einer vergangenen Ära
veröffentlichte er seine Autobiografie unter
dem treffenden Titel *En habillant l'époque*.

Die Marke Lanvin sah sich mit keinerlei
solcher Probleme konfrontiert.
Als besonnene, kluge Geschäftsfrau
hatte Jeanne Lanvin ihr Vermögen und
ihre finanzielle Unabhängigkeit geduldig
aufgebaut. Ihre Einkommensströme hatte
sie breit aufgestellt, um dem Auf und Ab
der Modewelt nicht ausgeliefert zu sein.
Zu Beginn des neuen Jahrzehnts war
Jeanne Lanvin bereits über 60 und hatte,
angefangen mit ihren Lehrjahren, ganze
50 Jahre in der Modebranche hinter sich.
Selbst so viele Jahre später blickte sie
nicht nostalgisch zurück, sondern malte
sich aus, welche Innovation noch in der
Zukunft liegen könnte. Wie eh und je erfand
sie die Mode neu und entwarf zeitgemäße
Kleider, die sie auf die Erwartungen und
Wünsche ihrer Kundinnen zuschnitt.
Währenddessen wagte sie sich weiterhin
an neue Unterfangen und Abenteuer, wie
etwa das Entwerfen von Kostümen für die
Filmbranche. Durch den Erfolg von Arpège
ermutigt, brachte sie gemeinsam mit André
Fraysse, der viele der berühmten Lanvin-
Parfums kreiert hatte, weitere Düfte auf den
Markt. Auf die 1933 kreierten Düfte *Scandal*
und *Eau de Lanvin* folgten 1934 *Rumeur*
und 1937 *Prétexte*. Das Parfumgeschäft,
das in den zwanziger Jahren lediglich ein
Wunschtraum gewesen war, wandelte sich
in den dreißiger Jahren in eine lukrative
Sparte für das Haus Lanvin. Jeannes Mühen
wurden wieder einmal von Erfolg gekrönt.

Evening dress, 1937.

Abendkleid, 1937.

p. 169:
Evening dress, 1938.

S. 169: Abendkleid, 1938.

CONSTANTLY REINVENTING FASHION / UNERMÜDLICHES NEUERFINDEN (1930-1939)

Summer dress with
embroidered sleeves,
1936.

Sommerkleid mit
bestickten Ärmeln,
1936.

p. 171: *Fusée* („rocket"
in French) summer dress,
1939.

S. 171: Sommerkleid
„Fusée"(„Rakete"), 1939.

The trend in fashion in the 1930s embodied a certain restraint, reflecting a break with the euphoria and wild exuberance of the previous decade. The slim, elongated silhouette had taken hold, although in Jeanne Lanvin's designs there was more volume in the sleeves. She sometimes seemed to draw her inspiration from religious attire and from an idealised vision of medieval court dress. At the same time, dresses and skirts, especially those for the summer season, were rapidly getting shorter, reaching the middle of the knee, an audacity that would have been unthinkable at the beginning of the 20th century. Here again, Jeanne Lanvin silently contributed to the emancipation of women by designing clothes that freed them from the shackles of the past while enhancing them, like the *Frivole dress* (1937), a light summer model with short, puffed sleeves that widened the shoulders and thus counterbalanced the very slender silhouette.

Die Modetrends der dreißiger Jahre waren Ausdruck einer gewissen Zurückhaltung und spiegelten den Bruch mit der Euphorie und dem Überschwang der Zwanziger wider. Eine schmale, längliche Silhouette hatte sich durchgesetzt. Jeanne Lanvins Kreationen zeichneten sich jedoch durch voluminösere Ärmel aus. Womöglich hatte sie sich dafür von kirchlichen Gewändern und einer idealisierten Version höfischer Kleider des Mittelalters inspirieren lassen. Gleichzeitig wurden Kleider und Röcke immer kürzer und kürzer, insbesondere in der Sommersaison, bis der Saum das Knie erreichte – eine so wagemutige Garderobe wäre Anfang des 20. Jahrhunderts noch undenkbar gewesen. Wieder einmal trug Jeanne Lanvin ohne viel Aufhebens zur Emanzipation der Frau bei, indem sie Kleider entwarf, die sie aus den Fesseln der Vergangenheit befreiten und die Frauen hingegen bestärkten. So zum Beispiel das Modell *Frivole* von 1937, ein leichtes Sommerkleid mit kurzen Puffärmeln, das die Schultern breiter wirken ließ und somit die sehr schmale Silhouette ausglich.

Frivole, Fugitive, and *Impromptu* dresses (sketches), 1937-1938.

Kleider „Frivole", „Fugitive" und „Impromptu" (Skizzen), 1937-1938.

FRIVOLE

pp. 174-175: Jeanne
Lanvin regularly drew
her inspiration from
liturgical garments,
as can be seen in these
two evening ensembles
dated 1935-1936.

S. 174-175: Jeanne
Lanvin ließ sich immer
wieder von liturgischen
Gewändern inspirieren,
wie an diesen von 1935
oder 1936 stammenden
Abendoutfits gut
zu erkennen ist.

p. 176: Winter coat, 1936.

S. 176: Wintermantel,
1936.

p. 177: *Lohengrin* coat,
1931.

S. 177: Mantel „Lohengrin",
1931.

However, the extreme elegance of the designs and the joyful modernity that emanated from them stood in contrast to the increasing struggles of Jeanne Lanvin and her family during those years and the increasingly alarming international situation. While she remained as busy as ever, Jeanne Lanvin's eyesight was deteriorating: she now had to wear glasses to focus on details. More worryingly, she suffered from diabetes, which required her to take insulin, a new medication that had been discovered just a couple of years before. Her daughter Marie-Blanche was overworked by the demands of her artistic career, and experienced chronic depression. A succession of deaths also afflicted Jeanne during those years, above all that of her beloved sister, Marie-Alix, in 1934, followed in 1936 by that of Jean Patou, a well-respected colleague, and finally that of Armand-Albert Rateau, the much-valued interior designer, in 1938. In France, democracy had been threatened on the night of 6 February 1934 when monarchist groups and far-right veterans, angered by scandals plaguing the Republic, tried to march on Parliament seeking its dissolution. Two years later, a devastating civil war ravaged Spain, a country dear to Jeanne Lanvin and where she owned boutiques in Madrid and Barcelona. The conflict had suddenly fuelled tensions between democratic countries and authoritarian regimes whose influence had spread across Europe. In France, a general strike paralysed the country in the spring of 1936 and led to progressive social reforms under the leadership of the Front Populaire, an alliance of left-leaning parties. Jeanne Lanvin, who had not forgotten her poverty-stricken origins and her difficult beginnings as an apprentice, endorsed the social reforms introduced by the Front Populaire, but was disappointed when Léon Blum's government backed down on the right of women to vote, which would not be granted until 1945.

Diese eleganten Entwürfe und der freudige Geist der Moderne, den sie ausstrahlten, standen im Gegensatz zur besorgniserregenden Weltlage und den wachsenden Schwierigkeiten, denen sich Jeanne Lanvin und ihre Familie während dieser Jahre stellen mussten. Zwar hatte Jeanne Lanvin so viel Arbeit wie nie zuvor, doch ihre Augen verschlechterten sich. Von nun an musste sie eine Brille tragen, um kleine Details erkennen zu können. Sie war außerdem an Diabetes erkrankt und musste Insulin nehmen, das erst wenige Jahre zuvor entdeckt worden war. Ihre Tochter Marie-Blanche litt, überwältigt von den Anforderungen ihrer Künstlerkarriere, an einer chronischen Depression. Dazu kamen mehrere Todesfälle, die Jeanne verkraften musste, insbesondere den Tod ihrer geliebten Schwester Marie-Alix im Jahr 1934. Jean Patou, ein geschätzter Kollege, starb 1936. Und schließlich starb 1938 der von ihr so geachtete Innenarchitekt Armand-Albert Rateau. In der Nacht des 6. Februar 1936 kam es zu einem Angriff auf die französische Demokratie, als Monarchisten und rechte Kriegsveteranen, erbost über die anhaltenden Skandale, zum Parlament marschierten, um es aufzulösen. Zwei Jahre später wütete ein furchtbarer Bürgerkrieg in Spanien – ein Land, dem sich Jeanne Lanvin sehr verbunden fühlte und in dem sie zwei Boutiquen besaß, eine in Madrid und eine in Barcelona. Der Konflikt hatte die Spannungen zwischen demokratischen Ländern und autoritären Regimen, deren Einfluss sich über ganz Europa erstreckte, weiter angeheizt. Ein Generalstreik legte im Frühling 1936 ganz Frankreich lahm und erwirkte eine progressive Sozialreform unter der Führung der Front Populaire, einem Zusammenschluss verschiedener linker Parteien. Jeanne Lanvin, die sich noch gut an die Armut ihrer Kindheit und ihre mühsamen Anfänge als Lehrling erinnerte, unterstützte die von der Front Populaire eingeführten Reformen, war jedoch enttäuscht, als Léon Blums Regierung das Frauenwahlrecht nicht einführte. Erst 1945 sollte Jeanne Lanvin das Wahlrecht erhalten.

Bodice with beaded decorations and skirt, 1938.

Rumpf mit Schmuckperlen und Rock, 1938

In 1935, she was invited to take part in the inaugural voyage of the *Normandie*, the new, luxurious flagship of the French transatlantic fleet, but Jeanne Lanvin was too tired to undertake the journey from Le Havre to New York. Dresses from her collections, however, were presented on board as part of a promotion of haute couture and were hailed by the American public. She preferred to devote herself to theatrical costumes for her friends Jean Cocteau, Jean Giraudoux and Louis Jouvet. Her knowledge of costume history had also led her to design dresses for Gina Manès, who played the role of Joséphine de Beauharnais in Abel Gance's film *Napoléon*. Jeanne Lanvin had been quick to understand the powerful promotional role that cinema could play in promoting haute couture, as she explained in straightforward terms during an interview with *Le Figaro* in 1932: "Couture is not an abstract art. We create a dress for a woman, a type of dress for a type of woman, and the beauty of fashion is above all inspired by the fashionable beauties...In this respect, the influence of cinema has been considerable. Cinema has enriched our inspiration by portraying, on countless screens, the living archetype of the modern woman."

1935 wurde Jeanne Lanvin auf die Jungfernfahrt der *Normandie*, dem neuen, luxuriös ausgestatteten Flaggschiff der transatlantischen französischen Flotte eingeladen. Sie war jedoch zu erschöpft, um sich auf die Reise von Le Havre nach New York zu begeben. Um für die französische Haute Couture zu werben, wurden Kleider aus ihren Kollektionen an Bord ausgestellt, die von den Amerikanern in den höchsten Tönen gelobt wurden. Jeanne Lanvin arbeitete währenddessen an Kostümen für die Theaterstücke ihrer Freunde Jean Cocteau, Jean Giraudoux und Louis Jouvet. Dank ihres historischen Modewissens kam sie dazu, Kostüme für Gina Manès zu entwerfen, die die Rolle der Joséphine de Beauharnais in Abel Gances Film *Napoléon* spielte. Jeanne Lanvin hatte schnell verstanden, welch wichtige Rolle Filme bei der Vermarktung von Haute Couture spielen könnten. Das erklärte sie in einem Interview

mit dem *Figaro* im Jahr 1932: „Das Nähen ist keine abstrakte Kunst. Man erschafft ein Kleid für eine Frau, einen bestimmten Kleidertyp für einen bestimmten Frauentyp, und die Schönheit der Mode wird vor allem von modischen Schönheiten geprägt... In diesem Sinne hat uns die Filmkunst sehr beeinflusst. Indem sie auf zahlreichen Leinwänden ein lebendiges Abbild der modernen Frau zeigt, hat sie unsere Inspiration enorm bereichert."

p. 180: Actress Gina Manès playing Joséphine de Beauharnais in Abel Gance's movie *Napoléon*. Her Empire-style dress was designed by Jeanne Lanvin.

S. 180: Schauspielerin Gina Manès als Joséphine de Beauharnais in Abel Gances Film *Napoléon*. Ihr Empire-Kleid wurde von Jeanne Lanvin entworfen.

Models wearing evening dresses, 1934.

Modelle in Abendkleidern, 1934.

Hat and evening dress, 1936.

Hut und Abendkleid, 1936.

p. 183: Sailor-inspired evening ensemble, 1937.

S. 183: Von Matrosenuniformen inspiriertes Abendoutfit, 1937.

CONSTANTLY REINVENTING FASHION / UNERMÜDLICHES NEUERFINDEN (1930-1939)

In 1938, an official visit by King George VI
of England gave Jeanne Lanvin the
opportunity to revive an early skill:
the French government had decided
to present the young princesses Elizabeth
and Margaret, who were not travelling with
their parents, with two dolls, France and
Marianne, whose wardrobe was created
by the country's greatest couturiers. Dresses
by Lanvin were prominently displayed.
Was it this prestigious assignment that had
prompted Jeanne Lanvin to create a dress
to clothe an angel for the 1939 World's Fair
in New York? The angel-winged mannequin,
halfway between a surrealist artwork and a
Gothic cathedral sculpture, was one of the
attractions of that fair, the last international
event in which Jeanne Lanvin exhibited,
along with the Golden Gate International
Exposition in San Francisco, which had
taken place at almost the same time.

1938, als der englische König George VI
zum Staatsbesuch nach Frankreich kam,
hatte Jeanne Lanvin Gelegenheit, ihre
Fähigkeiten von früher wieder aufleben zu
lassen. Die französische Regierung hatte
beschlossen, den jungen Prinzessinnen
Elizabeth und Margaret, die nicht mit nach
Frankreich gereist waren, zwei Puppen
namens France und Marianne zu schenken.
Deren Garderobe sollte von den besten
Modeschöpfern des Landes stammen –
und Kleider von Lanvin waren natürlich mit
von der Partie. Hatte diese prestigeträchtige
Aufgabe Jeanne Lanvin veranlasst, für die
Weltausstellung in New York 1939 das Kleid
für einen Engel zu entwerfen? Die Puppe
mit Engelsflügeln, halb surrealistisches
Kunstwerk, halb gotische Skulptur,
war jedenfalls eine riesige Attraktion.
Die Weltausstellung und die gleichzeitig
stattfindende Golden Gate International
Exposition in San Francisco waren die
letzten internationalen Veranstaltungen,
bei denen Jeanne Lanvin etwas ausstellte.

A fairy-tale like mansion
Die Märchenvilla

After several changes of residence in Paris, in 1920 Jeanne Lanvin acquired the former mansion of the Marquise Arconati-Visconti, located at 16, rue Barbet-de-Jouy, in the heart of Paris's select seventh arrondissement. The mansion had been built in the neoclassical style popular in the early 19th century and consisted of a single square building. She decided to retain the existing mansion as it was, with the exception of minor changes to the interior design, but instead added a new wing. The original building was offered as a residence to her daughter and her new son-in-law, Count Jean de Polignac, while she planned to use the new wing for her personal use. The construction, for which she commissioned the architect Richard Bouwens, was surely the most sumptuous of Jeanne Lanvin's property projects and an indication of the financial wealth she had reached by then. This mansion soon became Jeanne Lanvin's favourite retreat, the place where she met daily with her cherished daughter and her new son-in-law. While enjoying the peace and quiet of her own wing, she was able to take part in the social life of the couple and meet the musicians, painters and writers who gravitated around Marie-Blanche. The interior decoration was entrusted to Armand-Albert Rateau, a young designer and interior architect whom she had met through Paul Poiret in 1920. Rateau had distinguished himself in the design of the Daunou theatre in 1921, which belonged to Jeanne's close friend, Jane Renouardt. Rateau was initially asked to decorate a new dining room in the mansion's old part. Soon afterwards, Jeanne Lanvin invited him to design her boutiques and to collaborate with her on the idea of diversifying her activities into luxury interior design. Unfortunately, Lanvin Décoration, as the new company was called, proved to be the only venture launched by Jeanne Lanvin not to be as successful as expected, due to the lack of a sufficiently wealthy and refined clientele. Despite this setback, Jeanne Lanvin and Armand-Albert Rateau maintained a close and fruitful cooperation. One of the reasons for this lasting professional partnership was that they shared the same aesthetic vision, one that merged and reinvented ancient and modern styles. While his sources of inspiration were quite eclectic – French classicism, extreme oriental furniture, Greek and Roman antiquity – Rateau succeeded in creating harmonious interiors, both sumptuous and original, which gave the impression of decoration built up over time. After the construction of the new wing had been completed, Jeanne Lanvin entrusted him with the interior decoration of all the rooms. A large hall, reminiscent of the noble residences of the 18th century, served as the main entrance. A guest room was located to the left and was later transformed into a home office for Jeanne. At the end of the hall, a lushly panelled staircase led to the two upper floors. On the right, a large door opened onto a study-library, followed by a large living room – where fashion shows were sometimes held –, both were decorated in a relatively classical style. In both rooms paintings from Jeanne Lavin's vast collection were displayed. As soon as her fortune allowed her to do so, she had frequently bought paintings by contemporary artists she liked: among them masterpieces by Auguste Renoir, Odilon Redon, Claude Monet and even Picasso, to name the most famous. She also owned one of the pastel drawings that Degas had devoted to the world of milliners, as a nod to her youth.

p. 187: Jeanne Lanvin's drawing room with paintings by Monet and Renoir.

S. 187: Jeanne Lanvins Wohnzimmer mit Gemälden von Monet und Renoir.

Jeanne Lanvin with her pet dog in her dining room.

Jeanne Lanvin mit ihrem Hund im Esszimmer ihres Hauses.

p. 189: General view of the dining room.

S. 189: Ansicht des Esszimmers.

pp. 190-191: Jeanne Lanvin's bedroom.

S. 190-191: Jeanne Lanvins Schlafzimmer.

Nach mehreren Umzügen innerhalb von Paris kaufte Jeanne Lanvin 1920 eine Stadtvilla, die vormals der Marquise Arconati-Visconti gehört hatte. Die Villa befand sich in der Rue Barbet-de-Jouy Nummer 16, mitten im feinen siebten Arrondissement. Das Haus war im Anfang des 19. Jahrhunderts so beliebten neoklassizistischen Stil erbaut worden und bestand aus einem einzelnen Gebäude mit quadratischer Grundfläche. Am Haus selbst änderte sie nichts bis auf die Inneneinrichtung, entschloss sich jedoch, einen zusätzlichen Flügel anzubauen. In den bestehenden Teil des Gebäudes sollten ihre Tochter und ihr neuer Schwiegersohn Graf Jean de Polignac

einziehen, während sie den neuen Flügel bewohnen wollte. Die Baumaßnahmen, für die sie den Architekten Richard Bouwens beauftragte, waren sicher ihr kostspieligstes Immobilienprojekt und zeugten von dem Wohlstand, den sie inzwischen erreicht hatte. Die Stadtvilla wurde bald zu Jeanne Lanvins liebstem Rückzugsort. Hier traf sie sich täglich mit ihrer Tochter und ihrem Schwiegersohn. So konnte sie in ihren eigenen Wohnräumen die Ruhe genießen und andererseits am Sozialleben des jungen Paares teilnehmen, wenn wie so oft Musiker, Maler und Schriftsteller, mit denen Marie-Blanche verkehrte, zu Gast waren. Mit der Inneneinrichtung beauftragte sie Armand-Albert Rateau, einen jungen

Designer und Innenarchitekten, den sie 1920 über Paul Poiret kennengelernt hatte. Rateau hatte sich 1921 mit der Innenausstattung des Pariser Daunou-Theaters, das Jeannes guter Freundin Jane Renouardt gehörte, einen Namen gemacht. Ursprünglich wurde Rateau mit der Gestaltung eines neuen Esszimmers im alten Teil der Villa beauftragt. Kurz darauf wurde er von Jeanne Lanvin gebeten, ihre Boutiquen zu gestalten, und schließlich arbeiteten die beiden gemeinsam an einer neuen Sparte für hochwertige

Innenausstattung. Leider stellte sich heraus, dass es Lanvin Décoration an kultivierten, zahlungskräftigen Kunden fehlte, so dass das neue Unternehmen als einziges unter Jeanne Lanvins zahlreichen Projekten nicht von Erfolg gekrönt war. Trotz dieses Rückschlags arbeiteten Jeanne Lanvin und Armand-Albert Rateau weiterhin gut und eng zusammen. Einer der Gründe für die langanhaltende Partnerschaft lag in ihrer ähnlichen ästhetischen Vision, in der altertümliche und moderne Stilelemente miteinander verschmolzen und neu interpretiert wurden.

Zwar waren Rateaus Inspirationsquellen recht eklektisch – französischer Klassizismus, außergewöhnliche Möbelstücke aus Fernost, griechische und römische Antike – doch es gelang ihm immer, harmonische Innenräume entstehen zu lassen, die sowohl pompös als auch originell waren und den Eindruck erweckten, im Laufe der Zeit so gewachsen zu sein. Nach der Fertigstellung des neuen Flügels wurde Rateau mit der Gestaltung aller Räume des Hauses beauftragt.

Es gab eine große Eingangshalle, die an die Herrenhäuser aus dem 18. Jahrhundert erinnerte. Links davon befand sich ein Gästezimmer, das später in ein Büro für Jeanne umgewandelt wurde. Über eine opulent verzierte Treppe am Ende der Halle gelangte man zu den zwei oberen Etagen. Auf der rechten Seite führte eine Tür zu einer Bibliothek, die zugleich Arbeitszimmer war. Daran schloss sich ein weitläufiger Salon an, in dem gelegentlich Modenschauen stattfanden. Beide Räume waren in einem eher klassischen Stil gehalten. Außerdem hingen hier einige Gemälde aus Jeanne Lanvins großer Kunstsammlung. Sobald ihr Vermögen es zugelassen hatte, kaufte sie immer wieder Gemälde zeitgenössischer Künstler, die ihr besonders gefielen, darunter Meisterwerke von Auguste Renoir, Odilon Redon, Claude Monet und sogar Picasso, um nur die berühmtesten Namen in ihrer Sammlung zu nennen. Außerdem besaß sie eine von Degas' Pastellzeichnungen, die das Hutmachergewerbe ihrer Jugend darstellten.

The first floor included a large, hemispheric dining room that opened onto a terrace, while the top floor formed Jeanne Lanvin's private flat, which consisted of a bedroom, a boudoir, and a bathroom. There is little doubt that Jeanne Lanvin chose every detail that composed the space. The bedroom was upholstered in an ultramarine blue slightly darker than the Lanvin blue, with white embroidery on the lower parts, featuring Jeanne's favourite motif, the daisy ("marguerite" in French), as well as palms and rosettes. The bed was arranged in an alcove, and the bedspread had the same decorative motifs as the walls, but with the addition of butterflies. Three Russian icons hung at the head of the bed in their gold holders. The lights and two coffee tables were made of patinated bronze, Rateau's signature material. The floor, covered with a beige carpet, brought a touch of light to the room, as did the sofa in the same colour. A bay window offered a view on the boudoir, which served as a link between the room and the terrace. In a quintessentially neoclassical style, the mouldings of the panelling were painted in gold, a colour that blended well with white and blue, without any one of the three shades really dominating. Glass display cases on the walls reminded close friends admitted to her boudoir that Jeanne Lanvin was a great collector of exquisite objects, and not only of paintings. The floor was made of black and white marble slabs, which gave the place a slightly solemn look.

Im ersten Stock befand sich ein großes, halbrundes Esszimmer mit Terrasse. Jeanne Lanvins Privatwohnung mit Schlafzimmer, Ankleidezimmer und Badezimmer lag im obersten Stockwerk. Ohne Zweifel hatte Jeanne Lanvin jedes Detail dieser Wohnung sorgfältig ausgesucht. Das Schlafzimmer war mit Stoffen in einem Marineton, der etwas dunkler als das Lanvin-Blau war, ausgekleidet. Die Stoffe waren im unteren Bereich mit aufgestickten Palmen, Rosetten und Jeannes Lieblingsmotiv, der Margerite verziert. Das Bett stand in einer dafür vorgesehenen Nische und die Bettwäsche griff die Motive der Wand auf. Lediglich Schmetterlinge waren noch dazugekommen. An der Wand über dem Bett

hingen drei russische Ikonen in goldenen Halterungen. Tischchen und Leuchter bestanden aus patiniertem Bronze, ein Material, das als Rateaus Markenzeichen galt. Der Teppichboden und das Sofa waren in demselben Beigeton gehalten, um dem Raum eine gewisse Helligkeit zu verleihen. Aus dem Ankleidezimmer, das Schlafzimmer und Terrasse verband, hatte man durch die großen Fenster eine schöne Aussicht. Durch und durch neoklassizistisch waren die Goldakzente, die eine harmonische Brücke zwischen Weiß und Blau bildeten, so dass keine der Farben zu dominant wirkte. In die Wand eingelassene Glasvitrinen zeugten davon, dass Jeanne Lanvin neben Gemälden auch wertvolle Gegenstände sammelte, die sie hier zur Schau stellte. Der Boden bestand aus schwarz-weißen Marmorfliesen, die dem Raum eine gewisse Feierlichkeit verliehen.

More than any other room, the bathroom embodied the "modest luxury" approach that had defined Jeanne Lanvin's life philosophy. The white, beige, and black marble floor was decorated with regular geometric patterns. The bathroom furniture was a slightly darker beige marble, while the taps and lighting elements were in patinated bronze. The walls were in stucco, with the exception of a bas-relief above the bathtub, which depicted a doe and a stag in the undergrowth. Nothing was left to chance, as even the bronze sconces and taps were shaped to represent floral and animal themes.

In this fairytale-like setting, Jeanne Lanvin spent the last twenty years of her life, from 1925 to 1946.

Jeanne Lanvin's boudoir.

Jeanne Lanvins Ankleidezimmer.

The bathtub.

Badewanne.

Mehr noch als die anderen Räume verkörperte das Badezimmer Jeanne Lanvins Philosophie des „bescheidenen Luxus". Der Fußboden setzte sich aus geometrisch angeordneten Marmorfliesen in Weiß, Schwarz und Beige zusammen. Das Mobiliar bestand aus Marmor in einem etwas dunkleren Beigeton. Die Wasserhähne und Leuchter waren aus patiniertem Bronze. An der Wand oberhalb der Badewanne prangte ein Relief, auf dem ein Reh und ein Hirsch im Wald zu sehen waren. Hier war nichts dem Zufall überlassen – sogar die Wasserhähne und Wandleuchter aus Bronze griffen Motive aus dem Reich der Tiere und Pflanzen auf.

In dieser märchenhaften Umgebung verbrachte Jeanne Lanvin die letzten 20 Jahre ihres Lebens, von 1925 bis zu ihrem Tod im Jahr 1946.

1940-1946

Facing adversity

Gegen alle Widerstände

When the Second World War began in September 1939, Jeanne Lanvin was already seventy-two years old, a venerable age when many of her peers were looking more to the past than to the future. She could easily have chosen to suspend the brand's activities and retire from the life of constant hard work she had led for over sixty years. But inaction was not in her nature. Her determination and resolute sense of duty was as strong as ever. Perhaps she also anticipated that other haute couture houses would close, which would inevitably attract new clientele to hers. Madeleine Vionnet and Coco Chanel would indeed close their houses upon the first days of the war, leaving hundreds of seamstresses and dressmakers out of work. Elsa Schiaparelli and Cristóbal Balenciaga would follow suit in July 1940, at the beginning of France's occupation by German troops. Jeanne Lanvin could have retreated to Spain, a country where she had boutiques in Barcelona and Madrid, or to the United States, where she knew she would be celebrated, or even to Buenos Aires, since wealthy Argentine women were among her loyal clients. But she preferred to stay in Paris, at the heart of her world, as she had done during the previous war. Perhaps this decision was due to her increased difficulty in walking and moving, which would make any long journey perilous.

Als im September 1939 der zweite Weltkrieg ausbracht, war Jeanne Lanvin bereits 72 Jahre alt – ein Alter, in dem viele zurückschauen, statt den Blick in die Zukunft zu richten. Nachdem sie 60 Jahre lang unermüdlich gearbeitet hatte, hätte sie durchaus in den Ruhestand eintreten und das Modehaus vorübergehend schließen können. Doch Untätigkeit entsprach nicht ihrem Naturell. Sie war entschlossen und pflichtbewusst wie eh und je. Möglicherweise rechnete sie zudem mit der kriegsbedingten Schließung anderer Modehäuser, was unweigerlich mehr Kundschaft für Lanvin bedeutet hätte. Und tatsächlich schlossen Madeleine Vionnet und Coco Chanel ihre Modehäuser schon in den ersten Kriegstagen, so dass hunderte Näherinnen und Schneiderinnen ohne Arbeit dastanden. Im Juli 1940, als die deutschen Truppen Frankreich besetzten, folgten auch Elsa Schiaparelli und Cristóbal Balenciaga. Jeanne Lanvin hätte sich nach Spanien, wo sie zwei Boutiquen unterhielt, zurückziehen können, oder auch in die USA, wo man sie gefeiert hätte, oder sogar nach Buenos Aires, da die wohlhabenden Argentinierinnen treue Kundinnen von ihr waren. Doch wie schon im vorherigen Krieg blieb sie in Paris, im Mittelpunkt ihres Universums. Möglicherweise wurde sie in dieser Entscheidung auch dadurch beeinflusst, dass ihr das Laufen zunehmend schwer fiel. Eine lange Reise wäre womöglich zu gefährlich für sie gewesen.

Housecoat, 1946.

Hausmantel, 1946.

At the announcement of a new war, the mood of French society was sombre and disillusioned, far from the jubilation that had prevailed in July 1914. This heavy atmosphere was reflected in the names Jeanne Lanvin gave her designs: "Abri" (shelter), "Alerte" (alarm), "Attente" (wait), words that perfectly reflected the growing anxiety caused by a war for which France was not prepared. The defeat of the French army in May 1940 and the subsequent armistice in June quickly led to severe cutbacks on the supply of fabrics and other high-quality materials essential to haute couture, and the number of new models that could be presented per collection was lowered by the supervisory authorities from 300 to 100. Meanwhile, export sales, even to neutral countries such as Spain, were prohibited. Although she had to halve the number of employees due to the resulting lack of activity, Jeanne Lanvin refused to admit defeat and, as the saying goes, made something new out of something old, using fabrics from models in previous collections. However, at least until 1942, haute couture benefited from a certain benevolence on the part of the occupation authorities, as the very favourable exchange rate encouraged the wives of some German officers to buy clothes from the great French couturiers at bargain prices. In addition, the French collaborationist Vichy government granted privileged rationing tickets for clothes to its people, which allowed them to dress in the boutiques of Faubourg-Saint-Honoré.

Mit Ausbruch des Krieges war die Stimmung in der französischen Gesellschaft düster und desillusioniert – ganz anders als im Juli 1914, als überall gejubelt wurde. Diese Schwermütigkeit zeigt sich auch in den Namen, die Jeanne Lanvin ihren Entwürfen gab: *Abri* (Schutzraum), *Alerte* (Alarm) oder *Attente* (Warten). Diese Namen zeugen von der wachsenden Sorge angesichts eines Krieges, auf den das Land nicht vorbereitet war. Die Niederlage der französischen Armee im Mai 1940 und der darauffolgende Waffenstillstand im Juni führten schnell zu einem Rückgang der Stoffbestände, und auch andere hochwertige Materialien, die für die Haute Couture so wichtig waren, waren kaum mehr zu beschaffen. Die Anzahl neuer Modelle pro Kollektion wurde von den Aufsichtsbehörden von 300 auf 100 gesenkt, und Exporte – selbst in neutrale Länder wie Spanien – wurden untersagt. Obwohl diese Entwicklungen sie dazu zwangen, die Anzahl ihrer Angestellten zu halbieren, gab sich Jeanne Lanvin nicht geschlagen. Stattdessen schuf sie Neues aus Altem, indem sie Stoffreste von Modellen vergangener Kollektionen verwendete. Die Haute Couture profitierte zumindest bis 1942 von einer gewissen Nachsichtigkeit seitens der Besatzer. Der sehr vorteilhafte Wechselkurs veranlasste nämlich die Frauen einiger deutscher Offiziere, sich zum Schnäppchenpreis bei den französischen Luxusmarken einzudecken. Außerdem verteilte die südfranzösische Vichy-Regierung, die mit den Deutschen kollaborierte, Kleidergutscheine an die eigenen Bürgerinnen und Bürger, so dass diese sich in den Boutiquen der Rue du Faubourg-Saint-Honoré einkleiden konnten.

There is no doubt that Jeanne Lanvin resented this opportunistic clientele, and the names she gave to her designs evoked the hardships of daily life, scarce commodities, cold and fear. Some of the dresses she designed were named after old French provinces, as if to underline her attachment to eternal France, or after famous French writers, to keep alive the flame of French heritage. Like other fashion figures, she understood that maintaining French elegance and lifestyle was a form of passive resistance: as long as French women took care of the way they dressed and looked, nothing could break the country's soul. Although the embroidery was more sober than in peacetime and fabrics were used a little more sparingly, the haute couture collections kept alive the spirit of stylish luxury and fantasy that they had always embodied. Without openly defying the Vichy regime, Jeanne Lanvin resolutely ignored some of its discriminative laws and, while risking an administrative closure of the company, kept on her employees of Jewish faith even though iniquitous regulations barred them from many professions. Luckily, she was able to rely on silent support within the circles of government, in particular on her former right-hand man, Jean Labusquière, who had worked for twenty years at her side. After being mobilised at the beginning of the war as a reserve captain, he had joined the cabinet of the new Minister of Defence, General Charles Huntziger, as soon as the armistice was signed, and followed him until the plane crash in which they both perished at the end of 1941. Furthermore, Melchior de Polignac, the brother of her son-in-law Jean, had had connections in nationalist circles long before the war, and some of his friends held important positions in the Vichy administration.

Ohne Zweifel widerstrebte es Jeanne Lanvin, diese opportunistische Kundschaft zu bedienen. Die Namen, die sie ihren Kleidern gab, erinnern an die Nöte des Alltags, die schlechte Versorgungslage, die Kälte und den Hunger. Einige ihrer Entwürfe wurden nach den alten französischen Provinzen benannt, wie um ihre Verbundenheit mit dem wahren Frankreich zu unterstreichen. Andere benannte sie nach berühmten französischen Schriftstellern, um das französische Erbe hochzuhalten. Wie auch andere in der Modebranche sah sie das Aufrechterhalten französischer Eleganz und Lebensart als passiven Widerstand. Solange die Französinnen weiterhin auf sich und ihre Kleidung achtgaben, konnte nichts die Seele des Landes brechen. Doch auch der sparsamere Umgang mit Stoffen und die zurückhaltenderen Stickereien taten dem Stilgefühl, dem Luxus und der Fantasie, für die die Haute Couture stand, keinen Abbruch. Ohne offenen Widerstand gegen das Vichy-Regime zu leisten, widersetzte sich Jeanne Lanvin einigen der diskriminierenden Gesetze und kündigte ihren jüdischen Angestellten nicht, auch wenn diese in vielen Berufen nicht mehr arbeiten durften und sie dadurch die Schließung der Firma durch die Behörden riskierte. Glücklicherweise konnte sie sich auf stille Unterstützung aus Regierungskreisen verlassen, insbesondere auf Jean Labusquière, der 20 Jahre lang als rechte Hand an ihrer Seite stand. Dieser wurde zu Beginn des Krieges als Reservehauptmann eingezogen und arbeitete nach Unterzeichnung des Waffenstillstands im Kabinett des Kriegsministers General Charles Huntziger, bis beide Ende 1941 bei einem Flugzeugabsturz ums Leben kamen. Außerdem hatte Melchior de Polignac, der Bruder ihres Schwiegersohnes, bereits lange vor dem Krieg in nationalistischen Kreisen verkehrt, so dass er Freunde auf wichtigen Posten der Vichy-Regierung hatte.

Jacket, 1940s.

Jacke, 1940er Jahre.

In this gloomy atmosphere, a bereavement struck Jeanne Lanvin's close circle: Marie-Blanche's husband, Jean de Polignac, whose health had been failing for several years, succumbed to illness in the autumn of 1943. As for Jeanne, age and war deprivations were beginning to take their toll, and she was finding it increasingly difficult to get around on her own. Nevertheless, with the help of a nurse, she insisted on going to her office every day from her Parisian mansion at 16 rue Barbet-de-Jouy or from her house in Le Vésinet. She tirelessly created new designs despite the material constraints imposed by the war, thus bolstering the morale of her employees by her example of endurance and her refusal to sink into apathy. As the prospect of an Allied landing grew closer, the names she gave to her collections became more explicit: hence, in the spring of 1944, she conceived a silk shawl with motifs in the colours of the French flag with the words "Liberté, liberté chérie" (Freedom, cherished freedom) written on it, like an incantation. These words, taken from the sixth verse of the *Marseillaise*, France's national anthem, were not simply a patriotic appeal, but the heartfelt cry of a courageous woman who had fought all her life to be free.

Handbag, around 1940.

Handtasche, ca. 1940.

pp. 204-205: *Liberté, liberté chérie*, shawl, 1944.

S. 204-205: Schal „Liberté, liberté chérie", 1944.

Mitten in dieser düsteren Zeit kam es auch in Jeanne Lanvins engstem Familienkreis zu einem Trauerfall. Ihr Schwiegersohn Jean de Polignac, der bereits seit einigen Jahren bei schlechter Gesundheit gewesen war, unterlag im Herbst 1943 seiner Krankheit. Auch bei Jeanne machten sich das Alter und die Kriegsentbehrungen bemerkbar. Es fiel ihr zunehmend schwer, selbstständig zurechtzukommen. Dennoch machte sie sich von ihrer Pariser Stadtvilla oder ihrem Haus in Le Vésinet aus jeden Tag auf den Weg ins Büro. Dabei hatte sie Hilfe von einer Krankenschwester. Unermüdlich arbeitete sie trotz der Materialengpässe an neuen Entwürfen. Mit ihrem Durchhaltevermögen und ihrer Weigerung, in Apathie zu versinken, war sie ihren Mitarbeitern ein Vorbild. Als sich die baldige Landung der Alliierten abzeichnete, gab sie ihren Kreationen eindeutige Namen. Im Frühling 1944 entwarf sie einen Seidenschal in den Farben der französischen Flagge, auf dem wie eine Beschwörung die Worte „Liberté, liberté chérie" geschrieben standen. Diese Worte, zu Deutsch „Freiheit, geliebte Freiheit", stammten aus der sechsten Strophe der französischen Nationalhymne *Marseillaise* und waren nicht nur ein patriotischer Appel, sondern der von Herzen stammende Ruf einer mutigen Frau, die ihr ganzes Leben lang für ihre Freiheit gekämpft hatte.

In the months following the liberation of Paris at the end of the summer of 1944, Jeanne Lanvin discussed her work in *Vogue* magazine. Her words sound like a testament, and a final statement on the vision that had directed her long creative career:

For years, the viewers of my collections have been pleased to recognise a "Lanvin style". I know that there has been a lot of talk about this, but I have never adhered to a genre or attempted to accentuate a certain style. On the contrary, each season I tried to grasp the imponderable floating in the air, guided by events, and to draw from it, according to my personal vision, a design that translates the ideal of the moment.

A collection necessarily reflects artistic trends that permeate memory, trends that seem most alive, most innovative, and most complex at the same time. Far from willing to repeat myself and submit to a preconceived idea, I trust my instinct and surrender to my inspiration. Since I like moderation, I do not admit excess or narrowness: I fear poverty of lines and dullness as much as heavy and shocking pomp.

Because moderation is one of my values, I have always reacted against what masculinises women by seeking to add grace and charm to femininity through varied shapes and new details. This does not prevent me from designing very sporty outfits, which fit the powerful gestures of modern sports. I admire the ardent and youthful life too much to systematically sacrifice, for the love of the dress, the divided skirt, or the knicker.

If my interpretation denotes a genre, a style, it is neither voluntary nor deliberate. Let us take the example of two painters of the past and present. Without pretentious comparison, and only to seek the explanation of this word "style", let us ask the same question about them. Was Renoir running after his own style, or restrained by it? Does Christian Bérard care about creating works true to Christian Bérard's style? Quite naturally, personality surfaces in any artistic creation, and I would even say that this personality, emanating from the individual in spite of himself, creates the work and brings it to the attention of all.

When your mind is oriented towards constant creation, everything that the eye records is transformed and adapted for that creative goal, whatever it may be. The work comes naturally to you, it becomes an instinct, a truth, a need, another language.

The "Lanvin style" is therefore just the set of the main lines that are characteristic of my designs and that can be found each season, though they are concealed under a new rhythm, under an unforeseen trend, and this trend is just fashion, whose quest and embellishment have filled my life."

Jeanne Lanvin died peacefully, of old age, in her Parisian mansion on the morning of 6 July 1946. She was buried on the 10th of the same month in the cemetery at Le Vésinet.

Jeanne Lanvin at her desk, working on
a new dress model, 1942.

Jeanne Lanvin an ihrem Schreibtisch bei
der Arbeit an einem neuen Entwurf, 1942.

Einige Monate nach der Befreiung im Sommer 1944 sprach Jeanne Lanvin in der *Vogue* über ihre Arbeit. Ihre Worte klingen wie aus einem Testament und eine letzte Erklärung der Vision, die ihre lange Karriere begleitet hatte:

Schon seit Jahren meinen viele, in meinen Kollektion einen ‚Lanvin-Stil' zu erkennen. Ich bin mir bewusst, dass viel darüber geredet wird, aber ich habe mich nie nach einem bestimmten Genre gerichtet oder versucht, einer bestimmten Stilistik zu folgen. Ganz im Gegenteil versuche ich mit jeder Saison, das Unberechenbare, das in der Luft liegt, einzufangen. Daraus versuche ich – meiner eigenen Vision entsprechend – Entwürfe zu kreieren, die dem aktuellen Ideal entsprechen.

Eine Kollektion spiegelt unweigerlich die künstlerischen Trends wider, die uns in Erinnerung bleiben; die Trends, die am lebhaftesten, innovativsten und komplexesten sind. Ich möchte mich in meinem Schaffen nicht wiederholen oder Vorurteilen unterwerfen, sondern vertraue stattdessen auf mein Gefühl und gebe mich der Inspiration hin. Das richtige Maß ist mir wichtig – ich lasse weder Exzesse noch Schranken zu. Ich fürchte Belanglosigkeit und Mittelmaß ebenso wie übertriebenen Pomp.

Da das richtige Maß ein wichtiger Wert für mich ist, habe ich auf Elemente, die besonders maskulin sind, stets mit verschiedenen Formen und verspielten Details reagiert, um weibliche Grazie und Ausstrahlung wieder ins Spiel zu bringen. Das hält mich jedoch nicht davon ab, sehr sportive Outfits zu entwerfen, *die den Bewegungen moderner Sportarten angemessen sind. Ich bewundere die leidenschaftliche Jugend zu sehr, um aus Liebe zum Kleid auf Culottes oder Hosen zu verzichten.*

Wenn meine Kreationen zu einem Genre oder Stil passen sollten, so ist das weder bewusst noch absichtlich so. Lassen Sie mich das am Beispiel zweier Maler erklären – ohne mich mit ihnen vergleichen zu wollen. Nur um den Begriff ‚Stil' zu erläutern, lassen Sie mich Folgendes fragen: Ist Renoir seinem eigenen Stil hinterhergelaufen, oder wurde er durch diesen zurückgehalten? Achtet Christian Bérard in seinem Schaffen darauf, sich an Christian Bérards Stil zu halten? Auf ganz natürliche Weise zeigt sich in jeder künstlerischen Arbeit die eigene Persönlichkeit. Ich würde sogar so weit gehen zu behaupten, dass diese Persönlichkeit, die ohne weiteres Zutun von jedem Künstler ausgeht, für das Werk verantwortlich ist und es erst zu etwas Besonderem macht.

Wenn die Gedanken ohne Unterlass um das künstlerische Schaffen kreisen, wird alles, was man sieht im Sinne der Kreativität umgewandelt und angepasst. Die Kunst kommt auf natürliche Weise zum Künstler, wird zum Instinkt, zur Wahrheit, zu einem Bedürfnis und zu einer anderen Sprache.

Der ‚Lanvin-Stil' umfasst also lediglich die groben Linien, die typisch für meine Kreationen sind und in jeder Saison zu finden sind. Sie verbergen sich allerdings unter einem neuen Rhythmus, einem unvorhergesehenen Trend – und dieser Trend ist es, der die Mode ausmacht. Ihr habe ich mich ein Leben lang verschrieben.

Jeanne Lanvin starb im Alter von 79 Jahren in den Morgenstunden des 6. Juli 1946 in ihrer Stadtvilla. Sie wurde am 10. Juli auf dem Friedhof von Le Vésinet beigesetzt.

1946-

Jeanne Lanvin's Legacy

Jeanne Lanvins Vermächtnis

Although Jeanne Lanvin was 79 when she reached the end of her life, no succession scenario had been planned and when she passed away, no one really knew who would take over the reins of the company. *La Patronne*, as she was affectionately called by the employees, had always run the house without considering who would take over after she died, even though she had been assisted for several years by Jean Gaumont-Lanvin, Marie-Alix's son, who served as managing director.

While he excelled in administrative matters, Jean lacked the creative genius of his aunt and was unable to take over the reins. Against all odds, Marie-Blanche decided to take up the challenge: as she had been a widow for several years, was in frail health, and had never worked before in her entire life, this sounded risky. However, she threw herself into the adventure with nothing more than the closeness she had always enjoyed with her mother and a sharp aesthetic sense. Her connections to the artistic world and her very modern spirit allowed her, like her late mother, to capture the essence of the times and reflect it in the brand's designs. She could also count on the flawless corporate structure set up by Jeanne Lanvin, which meant that even the most fanciful visions could be turned into dress designs.

p. 210: *White Time* dress by Antonio del Castillo, 1953.

S. 210: Kleid „White Time" von Antonio del Castillo, 1953.

Marie-Blanche de Polignac, Jeanne Lanvin's daughter.

Jeanne Lanvins Tochter Marie-Blanche de Polignac.

p. 213: Winter coat designed by Marie-Blanche de Polignac, 1947.

S. 213: Ein von Marie-Blanche de Polignac entworfener Wintermantel, 1947.

Obwohl Jeanne Lanvin zum Zeitpunkt ihres Todes bereits 79 Jahre alt war, hatte man im Vorfeld kein Szenario dafür ausgearbeitet. Als sie starb, wusste niemand, wer nun die Zügel in die Hand nehmen sollte. *La Patronne*, wie sie von den Angestellten genannt wurde, hatte das Modehaus geführt, ohne über ihre Nachfolge nachzudenken. Allerdings war Jean Gaumont-Lanvin, der Sohn ihrer Schwester Marie-Alix, seit einiger Zeit als Geschäftsführer an ihrer Seite gewesen.

Jean war zwar ein guter Direktor, doch fehlte ihm das kreative Genie seiner Tante, so dass er nicht übernehmen konnte. Überraschend beschloss Marie-Blanche, sich der Herausforderung zu stellen. Da sie bereits seit einigen Jahren Witwe war, gesundheitliche Probleme hatte, und noch keinen Tag ihres Lebens gearbeitet hatte, war das ein riskantes Unterfangen. Doch sie stürzte sich ins Abenteuer. Verlassen konnte sie sich nur auf die enge Bindung, die sie stets zu ihrer Mutter gehabt hatte, und ihren ausgeprägten Sinn für Ästhetik. Dank ihrer Verbindungen zur Kunstszene und ihrer ausgesprochen modernen Einstellung war sie ebenso wie ihre Mutter in der Lage, den Zeitgeist einzufangen und in den Entwürfen der Marke zum Ausdruck zu bringen. Sie konnte sich außerdem auf die von Jeanne Lanvin aufgebaute Firmenstruktur verlassen, die es möglich machte, dass selbst die fantasievollsten Visionen in Kleiderentwürfe verwandelt werden konnten.

p. 214: Evening dress, 1947.

S. 214: Abendkleid, 1947.

Où est la marguerite ? (Where is the daisy?) summer dress, 1947.

Sommerkleid „Où est la marguerite ?" (Wo ist das Gänseblümchen?), 1947.

Marie-Blanche was also wise enough to hire a talented Spanish couturier, Antonio Cánovas del Castillo (1908-1984), to rejuvenate the brand in the early 1950s, and then gradually stepped down due to her failing health. Born into a famous Spanish family, Antonio Cánovas del Castillo shared the same name as his grandfather, a brilliant politician who had even chaired the Council of Ministers in the late 1890s and was assassinated by anarchists. Antonio Castillo, as he was known in the fashion world, fled Spain in 1936 and trained in haute couture with Chanel, Schiaparelli and Paquin, before leaving for the United States in 1945 to work alongside Elizabeth Arden. After returning to France two years later, he was considered a rising star of the new generation, the equal of Cristóbal Balenciaga and Christian Dior. His love of theatre and cinema – Jean Cocteau was a friend – made him the ideal successor to the women of the Lanvin family. He ran the brand from 1950 to 1963 – it was even briefly renamed Lanvin-Castillo after the death of Marie-Blanche in 1958, up until Castillo's departure.

Marie-Blanche war außerdem so klug gewesen, den talentierten spanischen Modeschöpfer Antonio Cánovas del Castillo (1908–1984) einzustellen. Dieser sollte der Marke in den frühen 1950er Jahren einen jugendlicheren Anstrich verpassen, so dass Marie-Blanche angesichts ihres gesundheitlichen Zustandes zurücktreten konnte. Antonio Cánovas del Castillo wurde in eine berühmte spanische Familie hineingeboren und trug denselben Namen wie sein Großvater, ein berühmter Politiker, der in den späten 1890er Jahren sogar Präsident des Ministerrates gewesen war und schließlich von Anarchisten ermordet wurde. Antonio Castillo, wie er in der Modebranche genannt wurde, floh 1936 aus Spanien und wurde bei Chanel, Schiaparelli und Pacquin in Haute Couture ausgebildet, bevor er 1945 in die USA ging, um mit Elizabeth Arden zusammenzuarbeiten. Als er zwei Jahre darauf nach Frankreich zurückkehrte, wurde er schnell zum aufstrebenden Star einer neuen Generation, der auf einer Stufe mit Cristóbal Balenciaga und Christian Dior stand. Dank seiner Liebe zum Film und zum Theater – er war ein Freund Jean Cocteaus – war er der ideale Nachfolger der Lanvin-Frauen. Von 1950 bis 1963 stand er an der Spitze der Marke Lanvin. Nach Marie-Blanches Tod im Jahr 1958 trug die Marke bis zu seinem Weggang sogar den Namen Lanvin-Castillo.

Hats by Antonio del Castillo, 1961.

Hutentwürfe von Antonio del Castillo, 1961.

p. 217:
Summer dress, 1957.

S. 217: Sommerkleid, 1957.

The dozen or so artistic directors who succeeded one another until the early 2000s, talented as they were, failed to demonstrate the same creative genius as the founder. While remaining a highly regarded luxury house, Lanvin lost its position in haute couture to new names, despite its thriving ready-to-wear departments and perfumes. It wasn't until 2001 and the purchase of the brand by a Taiwanese businesswoman, Shaw-Lan Wang, that Lanvin returned to the top of the fashion world thanks to Alber Elbaz's creative genius. Born in Morocco to a French-speaking Jewish family, Elbaz was raised in Israel and studied design at Ramat Gan before training in haute couture in the United States. He combined a fascination for the work of Jeanne Lanvin with a multicultural identity that encouraged him to seek inspiration from a wide range of aesthetic sources. His talent allowed the oldest haute couture house still in operation to move confidently into the 21st century. And in spring of 2015, the first major exhibition devoted to Jeanne Lanvin, which also celebrated Elbaz's fifteen-year reign over the brand, was held at the Palais Galliera (Musée de la Mode de la Ville de Paris), where the public was given the opportunity to admire some of the original sketches from the 1910s to the 1940s, rediscovered in 1980 in the attics of the building at 22 rue du Faubourg Saint-Honoré. The brand's most valuable tribute to its founder is, however, undoubtedly the launch in 2008, of a perfume whose name, "Jeanne Lanvin", brings her spirit to life every day.

Ein Dutzend verschiedener Designer übernahmen bis in die frühen 2000er Jahre nacheinander die Führung. So kreativ sie auch waren, keiner von ihnen konnte an das kreative Genie der Gründerin anknüpfen. Zwar blieb Lanvin ein angesehenes Luxus-Modehaus, doch die Stellung in der Haute Couture musste das Unternehmen trotz erfolgreicher Parfums und einer florierenden Ready-to-Wear-Sparte an die Konkurrenz abtreten. Erst nachdem die Marke 2001 von der taiwanesischen Geschäftsfrau Shaw-Lan Wang aufgekauft wurde, kehrte Lanvin dank des kreativen Genies von Alber Elbaz an die Spitze der Modewelt zurück. Elbaz wurde als Sohn französischsprachiger Juden in Marokko geboren und wuchs in Israel auf. Er studierte Modedesign an der Bar-Ilan-Universität in Tel-Aviv und wurde anschließend in den USA in Haute Couture ausgebildet. Angesichts seines multikulturellen Hintergrundes und seiner Faszination für Jeanne Lanvins Schaffen dienten ihm die verschiedensten ästhetischen Quellen als Inspiration. Mit seinem Talent führte er das älteste aktive Haute-Couture-Haus selbstsicher ins 21. Jahrhundert. Im Frühling 2015 fand im Palais Galliera im Pariser Modemuseum die erste große Ausstellung über Jeanne Lanvin statt. Hier wurde gleichzeitig Elbaz' 15. Jubiläum als kreativer Kopf der Marke gefeiert. Besucher der Ausstellung konnten unter anderem Originalskizzen aus den 1910er bis 1940er Jahren bestaunen, die man 1980 auf dem Dachboden des Gebäudes in der Rue du Faubourg Saint-Honoré Nummer 22 gefunden hatte. Das bedeutendste Tribut der Marke an ihre Gründerin war jedoch ohne Zweifel das Parfum „Jeanne Lanvin", das 2008 auf den Markt kam und ihr Vermächtnis jeden Tag aufs Neue zum Leben erweckt.

Sketches of the winter 1963-1964 collection.

Skizzen für die Winterkollektion 1963-1964.

p. 219: Alber Elbaz, creative director of the Lanvin brand from 2001 to 2015.

S. 219: Alber Elbaz war von 2001 bis 2005 für die kreative Leitung der Marke Lanvin verantwortlich.

p. 220: Coat and evening dress, early 1930s.

S. 220: Mantel und Abendkleid, frühe 1930er Jahre.

p. 222: Evening cape by Antonio del Castillo, 1963.

S. 222: Abendumhang von Antonio del Castillo, 1963.

Acknowledgements / Danksagung

This book is dedicated the memory of my uncle Jean-Paul Leclerq,
who was curator of old fashion and textile collections
at Musée des Arts Décoratifs, in Paris, from 1994 to 2006.
His immense knowledge in this field, as in many others,
has always been a source of inspiration.

My gratitude goes to Nadine Weinhold, my editor at teNeues Verlag,
and to the entire team at the publishing house for their
constant support. I am also morally indebted
to our friend and copyeditor, Lee Ripley,
for her expertise in editing and love for fashion.

Last but not least, many thanks to my beloved wife Agata,
who designed the book and made it shine, literally.

Dieses Buch entstand im Gedenken an meinen Onkel
Jean-Paul-Leclerq, der von 1994 bis 2006 im Pariser
Musée des Arts Décoratifs als Kurator für alte
Mode- und Textilkollektionen arbeitete. Sein großes Wissen
in diesem Bereich sowie in vielen anderen war für mich stets
ein Quell der Inspiration.

Mein Dank gilt Nadine Weinhold, meiner Redakteurin im teNeues
Verlag, sowie dem ganzen Team beim Verlag für die ständige
Unterstützung. Auch meiner langjährigen Freundin, Kollegin und
Lektorin Lee Ripley gilt mein Dank für ihre Expertise und ihre Liebe
für die Mode.

Schließlich danke ich meiner geliebten Frau Agata,
die das Buch entworfen und im wahrsten Sinne des Wortes
zum Strahlen gebracht hat.

Picture credits / Bildnachweise

© 2023 teNeues Verlag GmbH

Texts: © Pierre Toromanoff, Fancy Books Packaging UG. All rights reserved.

Editorial coordination by Nadine Weinhold, teNeues Verlag
Production by Alwine Krebber, teNeues Verlag
Photo editing, colour separation by Fancy Books Packaging and Luczak Studio
Layout and cover design by Agata Toromanoff, Fancy Books Packaging UG

Translation into German by WeSwitch GmbH (Catleen Grötschel)
Copyediting by Lee V. Ripley (English text), WeSwitch GmbH
(Katherina Polig, Romina Russo Lais, German translation)

ISBN: 978-3-96171-442-1
Library of Congress Number: 2022950624

Printed in Slovakia by Neografia a.s.

Published by teNeues Publishing Group

teNeues Verlag GmbH
Ohmstraße 8a
86199 Augsburg, Germany

Düsseldorf Office
Waldenburger Straße 13
41564 Kaarst, Germany
e-mail: books@teneues.com

Berlin Office
Lietzenburger Straße 53
10719 Berlin, Germany
e-mail: books@teneues.com

Press Department
e-mail: presse@teneues.com

teNeues Publishing Company
350 Seventh Avenue, Suite 301
New York, NY 10001, USA
Phone: +1-212-627-9090
Fax: +1-212-627-9511

www.teneues.com

teNeues Publishing Group
Augsburg / München
Berlin
Düsseldorf
London
New York

teNeues